CAMBRIDGE
GEOGRAPHY
PROJECT

World Geography

Core Book

Andy Beaumont
St. Mary's School
Cheshunt

Jane Herrington
Acland Burghley School
London

Rob Wheatley
Langdon Park School
London

Series editor:
David Lambert

PUBLISHED BY THE PRESS SYNDICATE OF THE UNIVERSITY OF CAMBRIDGE
The Pitt Building, Trumpington Street, Cambridge CB2 1RP, United Kingdom

CAMBRIDGE UNIVERSITY PRESS
The Edinburgh Building, Cambridge CB2 2RU, United Kingdom
40 West 20th Street, New York, NY 10011-4211, USA
10 Stamford Road, Oakleigh, Melbourne 3166, Australia

© Cambridge University Press 1997

First published 1997

Design and illustration by Hardlines, Charlbury

Printed in the United Kingdom at the University Press, Cambridge

Typeset in Grotesque and Utopia

A catalogue record for this book is available from the British Library

ISBN 0 521 45697 5 paperback

Picture research by Marilyn Rawlings

Cover photo: Liaison/Robert Harding Picture Library

Note to Students

This book has been written to form the basis of your GCSE studies in Geography. The information and activities contained in the book provide the CORE of your course. We hope you will gain the knowledge, understanding and skills you need, in an enjoyable way. As you work through the course your teacher will help you to identify and make links with other examples and case studies from around the world, so that you can apply what you have learned to new situations.

The main aim of the GCSE examination is to find out how well you can apply what you know, and what you understand. There is further guidance on the examination on pages 154–159. The authors of this book also believe that Geography helps prepare students to understand the world they live in – as well as preparing them for examinations! This is why many of the activities contain questions asking you to think about how you feel about things, par-ticularly about the future. It is also why we include 'Thinking Geography' – five special sections on aspects of living in the world, which Geography should help us understand. They are included to make you think and to form the basis of extension studies.

David Lambert

Contents

WHY STUDY GEOGRAPHY?

One of the questions most commonly asked of Geography teachers by their students is: 'Why take Geography – what job will it get me?'

There are three good reasons for taking Geography.

1 *It's a subject you enjoy and are interested in*
Geography courses at GCSE cover a wide range of issues and locations. Research shows that to students of school age, issues such as care of the environment, protection of fragile landscapes and the effects of global warming are very important. You are much more likely to do well in a subject that you enjoy and are interested in than one in which you are not.

2 *Breadth and balance*
For most students, GCSE Geography will be their last experience of the subject. It will be one of about ten subjects they will study. Geography makes a contribution to your general education. Colleges and employers are impressed by applicants who not only have a good grasp of the area in which they are going to specialise but are also aware of what is going on around them, locally, nationally and internationally. A Geography course also helps develop such useful skills as questioning, problem solving and decision making.

3 *It can get you a job*
If you enjoy the course you may decide to specialise in Geography. Whether you follow the vocational route through NVQ qualifications or the academic route through A levels and a degree course, Geography can offer interesting employment opportunities. As the world's largest industry, the tourist industry provides an obvious outlet for NVQ courses such as Travel and Tourism. Degree courses might lead to employment in such areas as environmental protection or planning. However, it is interesting that the most popular areas of employment for Geography graduates are in administration and operational management, together with research, design and development. Both these areas reflect Geography's emphasis on investigating, decision making and problem solving.

▲ *Protecting the landscape.*

▲ *Knowledge of the wider world.*

*Why I chose Geography.
Kerry Marriot attended Langdon Park
School in Tower Hamlets, East London.*

▼ *Where Geography may lead you.*

I first developed an interest in Geography during Year 7. I think this was because of the variety within the subject. I chose GCSE Geography because I found the issues raised were interesting because they relate to the real world. At A level I found that I developed a preference for Human Geography, which I have continued to enjoy as an undergraduate at Kings College London.

I still find the subject as fascinating as when I first began to study it. I've kept this interest because it allows me to question ideas about the world and about people around me.

Once I've finished my degree I hope to follow a career in town planning.

Whatever your reason for choosing Geography, your main priority must be to make the most of the course and try to achieve your highest possible grade.

Activities

1 Visit your school's careers library and find out the possible employment prospects listed under Geography.

2 Conduct a 'content audit' of your GCSE geography course. To do this, follow these instructions. You need to work in groups of five.

* Take a piece of paper and write at the top the heading *GCSE Geography*.

* Under the heading make five columns:

Topic	Enjoy	Know nothing yet	Theme	Place

* Each person in the group then takes one of the five units in this book. For your chosen unit, identify topics you will be studying, and then complete the other columns.

  – Do you think you will enjoy the topic? Give a reason for your answer.

  – Do you know anything about this topic yet?

  – What is the main theme? That is, is it physical geography, human geography, environmental geography?

  – What places are studied in this topic?

* When you've completed the analysis of your unit, briefly inform the rest of your group of its contents.

Population Geography

FOCUS

This unit investigates questions and issues about the geography of people. The main ideas are summarised by the following focus statements:

- The world's population is not evenly distributed.

- Populations are not static. They change because of the interrelationship between birth rates, death rates and migration.

- Many countries are experiencing changes in their population structure.

To examine these ideas we include examples from around the world, but particularly from **North America (Canada and the USA) and Mexico.**

Population distribution

People are spread unevenly across the world. At one extreme is the Antarctic, where virtually no-one lives, while at the other is Macau, the most densely populated country in the world. This unit studies the reasons for the variations in population distribution. However, this distribution is gradually changing, as a result of different birth and death rates, and the migration of people in different parts of the world. These changes are very important, as a rising population may put increased pressure on a nation's resources.

▼ **Figure 1.1**
Population of the world.

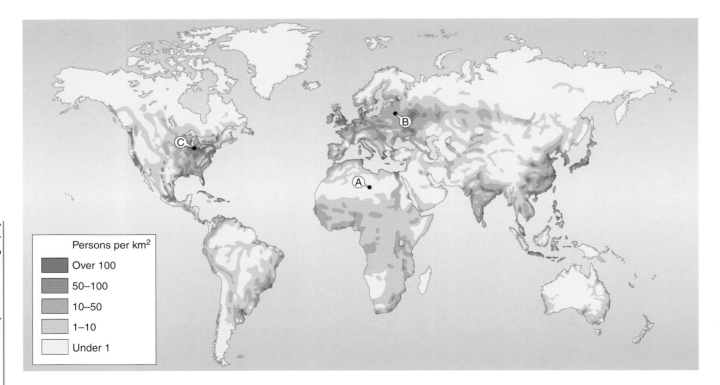

Persons per km²

- Over 100
- 50–100
- 10–50
- 1–10
- Under 1

Some countries are also concerned about their ageing populations. The migration of people can either be voluntary, as in the USA where people have moved to new areas of wealth, or forced, as in countries like Bosnia where people flee from war or persecution.

▶ **Figure 1.2**

One of the driest places in the world – the heart of the Sahara Desert in Algeria. The climate is inhospitable – it is too dry for people to live here permanently.

Activities

1 What is the population density at points **A**, **B** and **C** on **Figure 1.1**?

2 Use an atlas to name three areas of the world that are:

   a densely populated

   b sparsely populated.

3 For sparsely populated areas you have named, explain why few people live there.

4 Make a copy of the table below. Think about the physical factors that encourage people to settle in an area, and those that might discourage people.

Factor	Explanation	Example	Encourages/ discourages people
Low rainfall	Little water for farming	Sahara Desert	Discourages
River valley	Good soil for farming	Nile Valley	Encourages

Try to mention as many things as you can, such as the amount of rainfall and its seasonality, the height and relief of the land, natural hazards, etc. An atlas will help you locate places. What factors, other than physical ones, encourage people to settle in an area?

▲ **Figure 1.3**

A glacier in Alaska, USA. The climate and the terrain are inhospitable – it is too cold and too mountainous for people to live in this area.

Some patterns of population distribution can be explained by relationships between people's needs and the physical world, or environment. In the past this led people to believe in

► **Figure 1.4**
Selected statistics on population change.

	1950	1960	1970	1980	1990	2000 (estimate)
Africa						
Total population (thousands)	221,984	279,316	361,768	477,232	642,111	866,585
% world population	8.8	9.2	9.8	10.7	12.1	13.8
% increase over last decade	–	25.8	29.5	31.9	34.5	35.0
North America						
Total population (thousands)	220,361	269,565	321,036	373,767	427,226	479,393
% world population	8.8	8.9	8.7	8.4	8.1	7.7
% increase over last decade	–	22.3	19.1	16.4	14.3	12.2
South America						
Total population (thousands)	111,594	147,242	191,138	240,829	296,716	354,759
% world population	4.4	4.8	5.2	5.4	5.6	5.7
% increase over last decade	–	31.9	29.8	26.0	23.2	19.6
Asia						
Total population (thousands)	1,377,259	1,668,343	2,101,869	2,583,436	3,112,695	3,712,542
% world population	54.7	55.2	56.9	58.1	58.9	59.3
% increase over last decade	–	21.1	26.0	22.9	20.5	19.3
Europe						
Total population (thousands)	393,523	425,070	459,542	484,429	498,371	510,015
% world population	15.6	14.1	12.4	10.9	9.4	8.1
% increase over last decade	–	8.3	8.2	5.3	2.9	2.3
USSR/CIS						
Total population (thousands)	179,075	214,335	243,167	265,545	288,595	307,362
% world population	7.1	7.1	6.6	6.0	5.5	4.9
% increase over last decade	–	19.7	13.5	9.2	8.7	6.5
Oceania						
Total population (thousands)	12,647	15,782	19,329	22,799	26,481	30,144
% world population	0.5	0.5	0.5	0.5	0.5	0.5
% increase over last decade	–	24.8	22.5	18.0	16.1	13.8
World						
Total population (thousands)	2,516,443	3,019,653	3,697,849	4,448,037	5,292,195	6,260,800
% increase over last decade	–	20.0	22.5	20.3	19.0	18.3

environmental determinism. For example, the lack of rainfall in an area means that few people can live there. However, there are many occasions when such explanations do not work. For example, the desert area in south-west USA (see Figures 1.11 and 1.12) has an increasing population. There must be other explanations.

The pattern of population distribution is gradually changing. Between the years 1990 and 2000, a billion more people will be added to the world's population – but they will not be spread evenly around the globe.

Activities

Look carefully at **Figure 1.4**.

1 a Which continent has the largest population?

b Which continents have **(i)** an increasing, **(ii)** a decreasing share of the world's population?

c Which continent has the highest rate of population increase?

2 Write a report or produce a display which summarises the information in the table. It should include appropriate graphs and maps to show some of the information in the table more clearly. You could make use of line graphs and cumulative bars. Your report should also include the following:

• information on population increases – this will vary between continents

• notes on the changing share of world population

• examples of variations in percentage increases

• trends in the changing rates of population increase.

It may be possible to present all your work with the aid of a computer. You will need a word processor or desktop publishing package, a program that helps you to produce graphs and charts, and a program that produces maps.

How do populations change?

The population of a country changes because of the relationships between:

- the **birth rate**

- the **death rate**

- people moving into or out of a country (**migration**).

If more people are being born than are dying, the population rises. Where there is a high birth rate, the population increase is usually rapid, as in Mexico. However, if the death rate is higher than the birth rate, the population may start to decrease.

The number of births and deaths in a country affects its **population structure**. The shape of a population pyramid (Figure 1.6) shows whether there are a lot of young people in a country, or whether there are equal numbers in each age group, for example. The **median** is an average measurement of the age of a country's population – 50 per cent of people are older than this age, and 50 per cent are younger. In a country with an expanding population, the median age is usually low. In a country with a stationary population, the median age is higher.

▶ **Figure 1.5**

Population statistics for Canada, the USA and Mexico.

CANADA	Male		Female	
	Thousands	%	Thousands	%
Under 1	189.9	0.7	181.3	0.7
1–4	757.6	2.9	721.2	2.8
5–9	942.6	3.6	898.1	3.4
10–14	928.0	3.5	881.4	3.4
15–19	962.0	3.7	913.2	3.5
20–24	1,035.1	3.9	1,006.3	3.8
25–29	1,191.2	4.5	1,194.3	4.6
30–34	1,161.2	4.4	1,177.2	4.5
35–39	1,050.3	4.0	1,066.1	4.1
40–44	948.3	3.6	950.0	3.6
45–49	744.0	2.8	742.1	2.8
50–54	623.4	2.4	626.0	2.4
55–59	601.9	2.3	612.5	2.3
60–64	547.2	2.1	595.1	2.3
65–69	467.5	1.8	559.5	2.1
70–74	329.6	1.3	428.9	1.6
75–79	236.4	0.9	339.1	1.3
80–84	129.0	0.5	219.9	0.8
85+	79.2	0.3	181.9	0.7
Total population 26,218,500			Figures are for 1989	

USA	Male		Female	
	Thousands	%	Thousands	%
Under 1	2,020.0	0.8	1,925.0	0.8
1–4	7,578.0	3.1	7,229.0	2.9
5–9	9,321.0	3.8	8,890.0	3.6
10–14	8,688.0	3.5	8,261.0	3.3
15–19	9,092.0	3.7	8,721.0	3.5
20–24	9,369.0	3.8	9,334.0	3.8
25–29	10,865.0	4.4	1,083.0	0.4
30–34	11,077.0	4.5	11,057.0	4.5
35–39	9,731.0	3.9	9,889.0	4.0
40–44	8,294.0	3.3	8,589.0	3.5
45–49	6,600.0	2.7	6,921.0	2.8
50–54	5,509.0	2.2	5,867.0	2.4
55–59	5,121.0	2.1	5,605.0	2.3
60–64	5,078.0	2.0	5,788.0	2.3
65–69	4,632.0	1.9	5,539.0	2.2
70–74	3,463.0	1.4	4,548.0	1.8
75–79	2,386.0	1.0	3,647.0	1.5
80–84	1,307.0	0.5	2,422.0	1.0
85+	850.0	0.3	2,192.0	0.9
Total population 248,239,000			Figures are for 1989	

MEXICO	Male		Female	
	Thousands	%	Thousands	%
0–4	5,265.2	6.8	5,123.4	6.6
5–9	5,265.9	6.8	5,110.3	6.6
10–14	5,414.3	6.9	5,251.0	6.7
15–19	4,724.5	6.1	4,593.8	5.9
20–24	3,865.2	5.0	3,794.2	4.9
25–29	3,140.7	4.0	3,110.1	4.0
30–34	2,491.1	3.2	2,475.0	3.2
35–39	2,069.5	2.7	2,045.9	2.6
40–44	1,661.9	2.1	1,659.5	2.1
45–49	1,341.6	1.7	1,354.7	1.7
50–54	1,103.4	1.4	1,129.1	1.4
55–29	888.2	1.1	932.2	1.2
60–64	685.4	0.9	746.8	1.0
65–69	483.5	0.6	542.5	0.7
70–74	330.9	0.4	385.0	0.5
75–79	224.2	0.3	274.8	0.4
80–84	124.0	0.2	161.0	0.2
85+	70.7	0.1	96.5	0.1
Total population 77,938,288			Figures are for 1985	

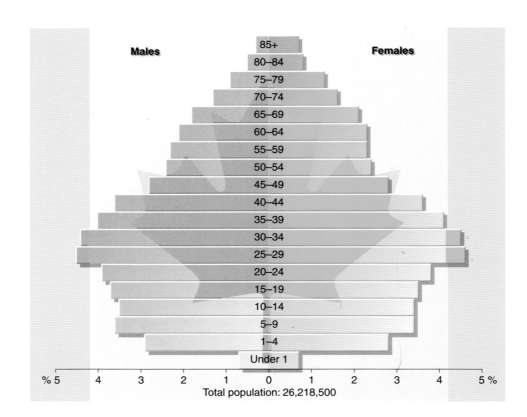

Males | **Females**

85+
80–84
75–79
70–74
65–69
60–64
55–59
50–54
45–49
40–44
35–39
30–34
25–29
20–24
15–19
10–14
5–9
1–4
Under 1

% 5   4   3   2   1   0   1   2   3   4   5 %

Total population: 26,218,500

Population pyramids

There are three basic shapes for population pyramids.

1 Expansive or 'true' pyramid
This is associated with rapid growth and a young population. Each age group is larger than the one above it. The birth rate is high compared with the death rate.

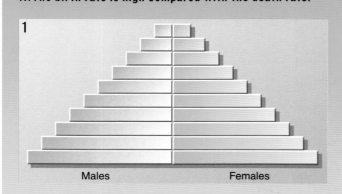

Males | Females

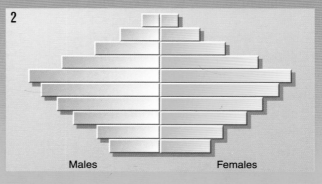

1

Males | Females

2 Constrictive
This has a low and declining birth rate and a low death rate. The median age of population increases and the population may become smaller.

3 Stationary
The proportion of people in each age group is equal. The population is neither increasing nor decreasing. This only happens when the birth rate and the death rate are both low, and constant for a long time.

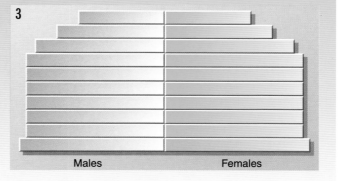

3

Males | Females

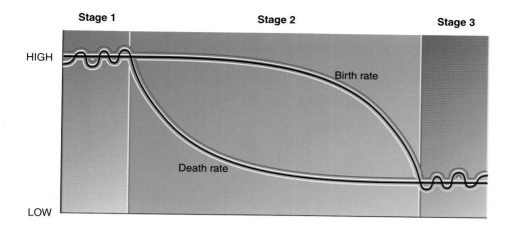

There are a number of reasons why population structures can vary between countries but it is usually because of variations in the birth rate. For example, the birth rate may be high because, for religious or traditional reasons, people expect to have a large family. Contraceptives (birth control) may be forbidden. In many countries children are seen as an economic asset because they can earn money to support their family. In countries where there are no state benefits, parents may want to make sure that they are cared for in their old age.

Advances in medicine have led to dramatic falls in the death rate around the world, and variations between countries are less significant.

By studying birth and death rates, geographers have devised the **demographic transition model** (Figure 1.7). The model has three stages:

Stage 1
Birth and death rates are both high. The population is stable.

Stage 2
The death rate falls but at first the birth rate remains high.
The population is growing.

Stage 3
Low birth and death rates. The population is stable, or growing slowly.

	1900	1910	1920	1930	1940	1950	1960	1970	1980	1990
USA										
Birth rate	33	30	27	22	20	25	23	16	16	15
Death rate	17	15	13	11	11	10	10	9	9	9
Canada										
Birth rate	27	34	29	24	22	27	27	17	15	14
Death rate	16	13	13	11	10	9	8	7	7	7
Mexico										
Birth rate	34	32	31	39	44	46	45	42	34	27
Death rate	33	33	25	27	23	16	11	10	7	5

◀ **Figure 1.8**
Percentage population change in the USA, Canada and Mexico, 1900 to 1990.

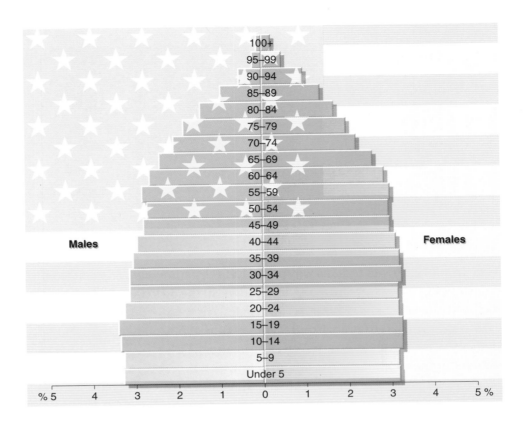

100+
95–99
90–94
85–89
80–84
75–79
70–74
65–69
60–64
55–59
50–54
45–49

Males   40–44   Females

35–39
30–34
25–29
20–24
15–19
10–14
5–9
Under 5

% 5   4   3   2   1   0   1   2   3   4   5 %

Activities

1 Write a short description of the population pyramid shown in **Figure 1.6**. Describe the overall shape, and the proportions of people in these three age groups:

   • young (< 15)
   • economically active (15–60)
   • old (>60).

2 Plot the population pyramids for the USA and Mexico using the statistics in **Figure 1.5**. Write a description of each diagram.

3 People over the age of 60, and those under 15, are often described as **dependants**. This means that they need someone of working age (15–59) to earn the resources to look after them. Calculate the proportions of people of working age and dependants in the USA and Mexico.

4 a Use **Figure 1.8** to draw a graph plotting the changes in population in the USA, Canada and Mexico between 1900 and 1990.

   b Suggest which stage of the demographic transition model each country has reached.

5 Suggest reasons for the increase in population in the USA and Canada in the 1950s. Why do you think this generation was known as the 'baby boomers'?

6 Why do you think Mexico's population rose so rapidly in the decade 1980–90?

7 Compare the population pyramid you have drawn for the USA in 1990 with **Figure 1.9**, which is the projected population structure for 2050. Describe the changes to the structure, and suggest some of the effects of these changes.

Population movement:
case study – North America

The countries of North America have population structures that are roughly stationary. The populations of Canada and the USA are increasing slowly, but important changes in the distribution of population are taking place. This is because of migration. Migration is the movement of people from one place of residence to another. This section investigates where people are moving to, and why.

▼ **Figure 1.10**

The USA at night. This satellite photograph shows the important centres of population. Use an atlas to identify California, Florida, Chicago, Detroit and other cities by the Great Lakes, and New York and Washington.

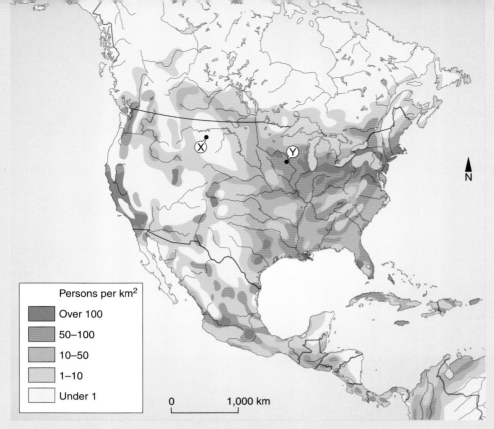

Persons per km²

	Over 100
	50–100
	10–50
	1–10
	Under 1

0   1,000 km

▼ **Figure 1.12**
Percentage change in population of North America, 1980 to 1990.

0   1,000 km

N

British Columbia · Alberta · Saskatchewan · Manitoba · Ontario · Quebec · Newfoundland
N.Brunswick · Price Edward I. · Nova Scotia · Vermont · New Hampshire · Massachusetts · Rhode Island · Connecticut · New Jersey · Delaware · DC · Maryland · West Virginia

Alaska · Yukon · N. W. Territories

Washington · Montana · North Dakota · Minnesota · Wisconsin · Michigan · New York · Maine
Oregon · Idaho · South Dakota · Iowa · Illinois · Indiana · Ohio · Pennsylvania
Nevada · Wyoming · Nebraska · Missouri · Kentucky · Virginia · North Carolina
California · Utah · Colorado · Kansas · Arkansas · Tennessee · South Carolina
Arizona · New Mexico · Oklahoma · Mississippi · Alabama · Georgia
Texas · Louisiana · Florida

Hawaii

0   200 km

Percentage change in population, 1980–90

	25+
	15.0 to 24.9
	5.0 to 14.9
	0.1 to 4.9
	−10.0 to 0.0

Baja California · Sonora · Chihuahua · Coahuila · Nuevo Leon · Tamaulipas · Campeche
Baja California Sur · Sinaloa · Durango · San Luis Potosi · Yucatan
Zacatecas · Nayarit · Veracruz · Tabasco · Quintana Roo
Jalisco · Colima · Michoacan de Ocampo · Guerrero · Oaxaca · Chiapas

1. Aguascalientes
2. Pueblo
3. Guanajuato
4. Queretaro
5. Mexico City
6. Tlaxcala
7. Hidalgo
8. Morelos
9. Distrito Federal

The ten fastest-growing cities by the year 1990

City	Population	% change
Fresno	354,202	62.9
Virginia Beach	393,069	49.9
Austin	465,622	34.6
Sacramento	369,365	34.0
San Diego	1,110,549	26.8
Charlotte	395,934	25.5
Phoenix	983,403	24.5
San José	782,248	24.3
Tucson	405,390	22.6
El Paso	515,342	21.1

Figure 1.13

The changing population of cities in the USA, 1980 to 1990.

The ten fastest-contracting cities by the year 1990

City	Population	% change
Detroit	1,027,974	−14.6
Pittsburgh	369,879	−12.8
St Louis	396,685	−12.4
Cleveland	505,616	−11.9
New Orleans	496,938	−10.9
Buffalo	328,123	−8.3
Chicago	2,783,726	−7.4
Atlanta	394,017	−7.3
Baltimore	736,014	−6.4
Philadelphia	1,585,577	−6.1

Activities

Study **Figures 1.11** and **1.12**.

1 What is the population density at points X and Y on **Figure 1.11**?

2 Describe the pattern of population density, referring to **densely populated** and **sparsely populated** areas.

3 Try to explain this pattern using only physical explanations (see activities on page 2). You will need to use an atlas. Organise your work under these headings:

  • relief and terrain
  • climate
  • access to coasts and navigable rivers.

4 Using **Figure 1.12**, describe how the population is changing in North America.

5 Plot the information in **Figure 1.13** on a base map of the USA. To do this, mark on your map, in different colours, the growing and shrinking cities.

6 How well does the pattern of growing and shrinking cities fit in with the information in **Figure 1.12**?

Places where the Cootes family have lived and worked.

▶ **Figure 1.14**
Central Valley, California. Note the contrast between the irrigated crops in the foreground and the dry hills in the background.

◀ **Figure 1.15**
Monument Valley, in the Arizona Desert.

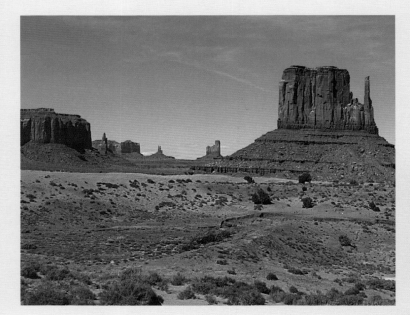

▶ **Figure 1.16**
Inside a steelworks in north-east USA. Locally mined coal and imported iron ore were traditionally used to make the finished product (steel).

Figure 1.17 *The Cootes family have a reunion.*

Activities

1 Plot the moves of the Cootes family in the USA by drawing arrows of their movements on a base map.

2 Explain how the following affected the Cootes family's decision to move:

   a changing job opportunities

   b climate

   c leisure opportunities.

3 Explain how technology has enabled large populations to grow in southern California and Arizona, where there is less than 500 mm of rain per year.

International migration

Migration occurs not only within a country, but also between countries. For example, there is a long history of movement of people between Canada, the USA and Mexico. The present populations of Canada and the USA are the result of migrations from across the Atlantic Ocean.

Between 1851 and 1951, Canada's population increased from 2.4 million to 14 million. It accepted 7.2 million migrants from Europe. However, during the same period 6.5 million Canadians migrated to the USA.

▶ **Figure 1.18**
A general push–pull model of migration. Make this model specific by applying it to an example of migration, for example the migration of several million Irish people to the USA during the 19th century.

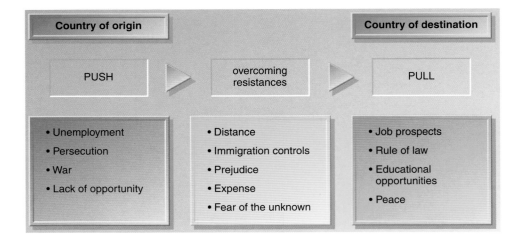

People may wish to move from one country to another for many reasons, for example:

- to find work (sometimes called economic migrants)

- to join members of their family

- to escape from religious persecution

- to escape from war

- to escape from natural disasters.

Reasons such as these can be classified into either 'push' or 'pull' factors (Figure 1.18).

There has been a considerable change in the countries that have supplied migrants to Canada and the USA in the past decades – see Figure 1.19.

Both countries operate an immigration control system. The Canadian system is based on a points system – see Figure 1.20.

Not all migrants enter the USA legally. Illegal immigration is a controversial issue in some areas of the USA. It is estimated that, in 1991, 3 million people crossed the border between the USA and Mexico, but only a third of them were stopped by

▼ **Figure 1.19**
Main countries of origin of immigrants to Canada and the USA.

Canada		USA
1951	1984	1992
1 UK	Vietnam	Mexico 22.0%
2 Germany	Hong Kong	Vietnam 8.0%
3 Italy	USA	Philippines 6.3%
4 Netherlands	India	Soviet Union 4.5%
5 Poland	UK	Dominican Republic 4.3%
6 France	Poland	China 4.0%
7 USA	Philippines	India 3.8%
8 Belgium	El Salvador	El Salvador 2.7%
9 Yugoslavia	Jamaica	Poland 2.6%
10 Denmark	China	UK 2.1%

police. It is impossible to guard this 2,500 km boundary between the world's most powerful country and its much poorer neighbour. A 3-metre high, solid steel barricade has been built on the busiest section, near San Diego (southern California). It stretches for 22 km, and at night is illuminated by powerful lights.

The USA is a nation built on immigration, and migrants used to be welcomed. But attitudes to immigrants seem to be changing. Many Americans think the country is being 'over-run' by immigrants. Their worries seem to be based on certain myths (popular ideas that are not always based on the truth). Here are three common ones:

- 'Migrants take other people's jobs' – in fact, migrants create jobs, by using services, and starting up small businesses. Many low-paid jobs are done by illegal immigrants, for example in restaurant kitchens, or driving taxis. Payment is often in cash, rather than through an official payroll. Migrants are often exploited as they become a 'servant' class of people.

- 'Illegal immigrants cross the border permanently' – in fact, most migrants return to Mexico, having worked in the USA for just a few months.

- 'Illegal immigrants put pressure on the welfare system' – in fact, they have few rights, and can be forced to leave if they try to claim benefits, as they have to identify themselves. 'We come to work, not to go on welfare,' said one migrant.

▼ **Figure 1.20**
Self-assessment work sheet for people wishing to move to Canada.

SELF-ASSESSMENT WORK SHEET

Factor		Maximum points	Your score
1	Age	10	
2	Education	16	
3	Specific vocational preparation (training/education/apprenticeship)	18	
4	Occupation (*you need a minimum of 1 point or arranged employment*)	10	
5	Arranged employment/designated occupation	10	
6	Work experience (*you need a minimum of 1 point or arranged employment*)	8	
7	Language ability	15	
8	Demographic factor	19	8
9	Personal suitability	10	6
10	Relative in Canada (bonus)	5	
Total			

Note: You must achieve a score of 70 points to qualify for an immigrant visa and should not apply unless you obtain a minimum of 60 points, bearing in mind that up to 10 points may be awarded by a visa officer for personal suitability.

Activities

1 a Which continent supplied the majority of migrants to Canada in 1951?

b Why do you think so many people wanted to leave that continent in the early 1950s?

2 a Which continent supplied the majority of migrants to Canada in 1984?

b Why do you think so many people wished to leave that continent in the 1980s?

3 a Which type of people would find it easiest to migrate to Canada?

b Why do you think Canada wishes to attract these people?

4 The following suggestions have been made to tackle the issue of illegal migration from Mexico to the USA:

- Remove benefits.
- Increase border controls.
- Help Mexico to develop its economy so that fewer people want to migrate.
- Do nothing, as the real costs are very small.

Write a letter to a newspaper about the issue, and say which of these suggestions you agree with, and which you disagree with. Give your reasons in each case.

THINKING GEOGRAPHY

The urge to draw boundaries

These two pages are about the 'political geography' of the world. Most of us know that almost all the land surface of the Earth is divided up into countries (see pages 21 and 22). The total number of countries is growing, and is now just over 200. The only continent without countries is Antarctica, because it is unable to support permanent human settlement. Even here there is competition between countries (e.g. Britain, France, New Zealand) to share out the territory, because of the mineral wealth that may lie beneath the land. However, in 1991 an international agreement banned all mining in Antarctica for 50 years. Thus the exploitation of that continent, the 'last great wilderness', is 'on hold'. Some people suggest that Antarctica should become a vast international wilderness park, owned by no one for the benefit of everyone. But can the governments of the world cope with a territory (land) without borders?

Visible and invisible boundaries

Even if Antarctica were to be carved up by competing countries, and thus acquire international boundaries, the continent could never become a real country (or collection of countries) in its own right, because it is unoccupied (has no permanent residents). *Countries* are a human invention: without people there can be no country.

There are many examples in history of cases where already occupied territories have been carved up by invading countries. We investigate the cases of North America and Africa on the next two pages.

FACT FILE: ANTARCTICA
- 14 million km²
- 90% of all the world's ice
- World's lowest temperature: –89°C at Cape Vostok

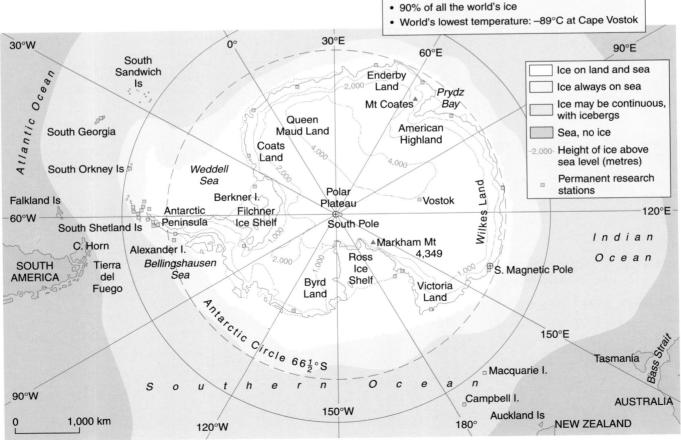

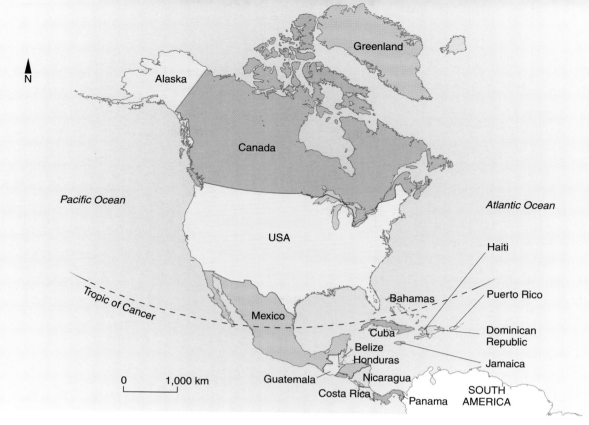

Political map of North America.

1 North America

First the Spanish and then the French and British left their 'cultural footprints' over the continent of North America. You only have to look at the place names on a large-scale map to see this. Many other groups have been influential too, including peoples from Africa and other parts of Europe. Native Americans were not as possessive of land as Europeans are, and they were almost totally destroyed (genocide) in the last century. Black Americans, most of whom are descended from Africans who were imported as slaves, still have less than a fair share of social and economic well-being in America. There are many diverse groups of people in Canada and the USA, and it is the function of these countries' governments to maintain their national identity by appealing to feelings of patriotism. For example, school students in the USA begin the day by demonstrating loyalty to the USA, and a flag is displayed in all classrooms.

2 Africa

European countries also imposed national boundaries on the peoples of Africa. Today there are 49 African countries (see map on next page), but some of their boundaries make no sense to the people who live there. Some of these boundaries were drawn without reference to the landscape or to the people who lived there, with the result that the boundaries separate some peoples who don't feel they should be separated. Other boundaries define countries that contain people from ethnic groups that have not been at peace with each other for centuries. Many African countries now spend huge sums of money on the defence of their borders, rather than improving the social and economic well-being of the peoples within their borders.

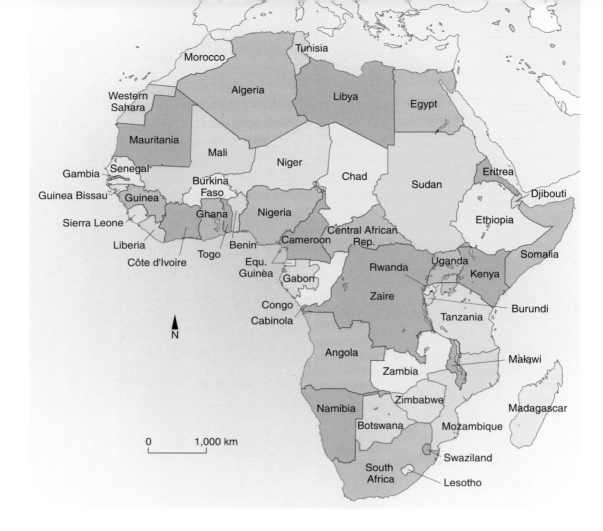

▶ *Political map
of Africa.*

Holding together and breaking apart

The USA successfully holds diverse groups of people together. A much smaller country, for example Rwanda in Africa, may be less successful. In 1991, the largest country on Earth, the Union of Soviet Socialist Republics (USSR), which was created in 1921 after the 1917 communist revolution, broke up into 15 different countries. After centuries of fighting and genocide, the countries of Europe are moving towards greater union (see pages 152–153), but critics from all parts of Europe argue that differences within Europe are so great that it will be impossible to create a truly successful United Europe.

A question of identity

When you fill in an application form to a college or university, what will you write in the box for 'Nationality'? For many of this book's readers the answer is: 'British'. That may be the correct legal answer – but how many students would prefer to write 'English', 'Scottish' or 'Welsh', or something else? Would it be possible to write 'European', or even 'None'?

Is your nationality defined by the country you live in? Or are there differences between the terms *nation* and *country* (or *nation-state*)? Such questions are important, and tricky to answer.

Distribution of the Kurdish people

GEORGIA
Black Sea
ARMENIA AZERBAIJAN
Lake Savan
Mt Ararat ▲
AZ •
Araxes
T U R K E Y
Lake Van
• Tabriz
Lake Urumiya
I R A N

0   200 km

CYPRUS
Mediterranean Sea
S Y R I A
Euphrates
Tigris
Beirut • LEB •
• Damascus
N
I R A Q
Baghdad •
AZ = Azerbaijan
LEB = Lebanon

Area that would become independent Kurdistan

GEORGIA
Black Sea
ARMENIA AZERBAIJAN
Lake Savan
Mt Ararat ▲
AZ •
Araxes
T U R K E Y
Lake Van
• Tabriz
Lake Urumiya
I R A N

0   200 km

CYPRUS
Mediterranean Sea
S Y R I A
Euphrates
Tigris
Beirut • LEB •
• Damascus
N
I R A Q
Baghdad •
AZ = Azerbaijan
LEB = Lebanon

▲ Territory of the Kurdish people.

A nation is when a group of people who are united by language and/or beliefs and traditions, associate themselves with a territory. They have a *moral claim* to 'their land', which results from their feelings of belonging. Such territory does not always have clear boundaries, because it may not have the *legal status* of a country. For example, the Kurds may describe themselves as a nation, but they occupy land that is legally part of Turkey, Iraq and Iran (see map, left).

This definition of *nation* is not an adequate definition of *country*. Very few countries are united by a common language, beliefs and traditions. Most are multi-cultural and multi-lingual, and many are multi-national (including Britain).

Nationalism

Most people need to belong to a cultural or national group. This is healthy, and can be described as a person's *first identity*. People also have a *second identity* as a member of their country or nation-state. There is nothing wrong with this, and some patriotic feelings are healthy too. However, some people develop such feelings in an unhealthy way. They exaggerate what they claim is 'good' about their nationality, and they exaggerate what they claim is 'bad' about other groups. This is the basis of nationalism.

It's important to understand that positive feelings of national identity do not inevitably lead to national*ist* feelings.

Activities

1 Study the text on pages 20–23. Design and write a one-page poster or leaflet for 12-year-olds to show the difference between a nation and a country. Use examples and illustrations.

2 a Examine your own cultural and national identities. Try to describe your 'first identity'.

  b Assume that your 'second identity' is British. In your own words, describe what it means to 'be British'.

The Geography of Settlements

FOCUS

This unit investigates questions and issues about where people live and how their settlements are arranged. The main ideas are summarised by the following statements:

- Urbanisation is a global phenomenon: it happens all over the world.

- Cities often have features in common because they have similar functions, e.g. providing services for people, like housing, shops, etc.

- Each city has unique features: there is only one London, and there is only one Paris.

- The way urban places are organised – who gets what, where,

and why – is usually contested (argued about).

- Quality of life usually improves as you move towards the edge of cities in the developed world, but the scale of a city map can hide differences in the quality of life.

- Some people can exercise more choice over where they live than others can.

To examine these ideas, several examples of urban places are referred to: London, Swindon, Los Angeles, Curitiba (Brazil), Paris and Cairo. In addition, a case study of the Yorkshire Dales is included to help us investigate rural settlement.

Quality of life in cities

The United Nations defines a city as a settlement with a population of more than 20,000 people. Cities cover more and more of the Earth's surface. An increasing proportion of the world's people live in cities (Figure 2.2).

◀ **Figure 2.1**
Europe at night. This night-time view of the lights of Europe shows the sheer density of population.

	1920	1940	1960	1980	1990
Europe	32	37	41	50	42
North America	38	45	57	61	75
Oceania	34	38	50	50	70
USSR	10	24	36	46	66
East Asia	7	13	20	28	34
South Asia	6	8	14	21	26
Latin America	14	19	32	41	71
Africa	5	7	13	18	30
World	14	19	25	32	42

◀ **Figure 2.2**
Percentage of the population living in cities in different continents, 1920–90.

It is possible to find very big differences between countries. In Germany, Belgium and Israel, for example, nine out of every ten people live in cities, but in Nepal, Malawi and Oman less than one person in ten lives in a city (Figure 2.3). In some countries, such as Mexico, China and Egypt, cities are growing rapidly whilst in other countries, such as the UK, cities are losing population .

Whether a city is growing or shrinking, they all have to serve the needs of their inhabitants. Throughout history, city dwellers have always been divided about the attractions of their surroundings, as the comments on London in Figure 2.4 show.

▼ **Figure 2.3**
World urbanisation.

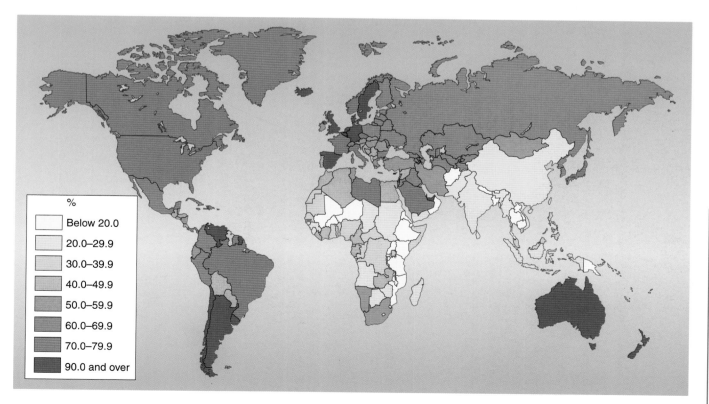

%
- Below 20.0
- 20.0–29.9
- 30.0–39.9
- 40.0–49.9
- 50.0–59.9
- 60.0–69.9
- 70.0–79.9
- 90.0 and over

Unit 2 **The Geography of Settlements**

'It's a great place. Immense, the richest town in the world, the biggest port, the greatest manufacturing town, the imperial city, the centre of civilization, the heart of the world.'
H. G. Wells, Tono-Bungay, 1909

'As vast as an ocean, the screech and howl of machinery, the railways above the houses.'
Feodor Dostoevsky, 1867

'Lovely Oxford Street, wide pavements and handsome glass windows allowed us to gaze at the splendidly lit shopfronts in comfort.'
A German traveller, 1867

'... when a man is tired of London, he is tired of life; for there is in London all that life can afford.'
Dr Samuel Johnson, 1777

'A wet Sunday in London, shops closed, streets almost empty, the aspect of a well-kept graveyard ... it is horrible.'
Hippolyte Tone, a French traveller in the 1860s

'Hell is a city much like London – A populous and smoky city.'
Percy Bysshe Shelley, 1819

'There is no such absolute loneliness as many have felt in London.'
Charles Heddon Spurgeon, 1834–92

'The very turmoil of the streets has something against which human nature rebels. Hundreds of thousands crowd by one another as though they have nothing in common.'
Frederick Engels, 1846

'£1,500 a month is not what people need for living in central London, and which I am more or less obliged to do.'
Lord Gowrie, 1985

'London life suits me excellently. I think the town and streets are beautiful.'
Felix Mendelssohn, 1829

▲ **Figure 2.4**
Some views on London.

All cities have things in common, and also features that make them unique. It is because all cities provide services such as transport, housing, shopping and employment that they often appear similar. Some people suggest that cities are beginning to lose much of their own character and are beginning to look increasingly the same.

But change is difficult to resist, as is shown by this extract from a detective story set in Venice. The character speaking is a local politician worried about the future of Venice.

> 'If the city survives at all, it will be as a theme park for rich tourists, as Veniceland, a wholly-owned Disney subsidiary with actors dressed up as the Doge and the council of Ten, with catering by McDonalds.'

Michael Dibden, *Dead Lagoon*, 1994

▼ **Figure 2.5**
Aspects of Paris and London.

River Seine

River Thames

Trafalgar Square

Paris Metro

The Louvre

London Underground

Activities

1 Draw a graph to compare the statistics in **Figure 2.2**.

2 Write a paragraph to describe and explain the trends shown by your graph.

3 Use the quotes in **Figure 2.4** to create two lists: one listing all the pleasant things said about the city, and the other listing all the unpleasant things.

4 Think of a city you know well. Imagine what the city could be like in 20 years' time. Think about such things as transport, work and shopping. Write one paragraph to say what you *hope* the city will be like and another to say what it will *probably* be like.

5 Make a copy of the chart below. Referring to **Figure 2.5** and other sources of information on London and Paris, complete the three columns.

Found in both cities	Found only in London	Found only in Paris

6 Explain why you think the character in the novel *Dead Lagoon* quoted on page 26 is worried about the future of the city of Venice.

Who gets what? The unequal city

Figure 2.6 shows the **gross domestic product** (GDP) per head for countries in the European Union (EU) and for the Standard Regions of the UK. The figures are an 'index', with 100 being the EU average. Presenting the figures like this helps us to compare them. As you can see, the UK is close to average in list (a), and the South East is high in list (b). It would seem therefore that life in London should be quite prosperous. However, these figures mask differences to be found *within* London. It is therefore important to study places at a variety of scales. Doing so makes it possible to detect uneven distributions within regions. As an example, we can examine quality of life in London (Task 2).

a GDP by EU country

Luxembourg	160
Belgium	113
Denmark	112
France	110
Germany	108
Netherlands	103
Italy	102
UK	99
Ireland	81
Spain	78
Portugal	69
Greece	63

b GDP by Standard Region

South East	116
East Anglia	101
Scotland	97
South West	94
East Midlands	93
West Midlands	91
Yorkshire & Humberside	91
North West	90
North	89
Wales	84
Northern Ireland	79

100 = average

◀ **Figure 2.6**
GDP in the EU and in the UK, 1993.

What is quality of life?

For some years now geographers have been interested in ways of comparing what life is like for different groups of people. They have tried to identify what is important to people. For example, most people would agree that having a home with basic facilities such as a bathroom and toilet is important; also being able to find work, to feel secure, and to have access to good health care. Such items are known as **indicators**. They can be used individually or they can be grouped together to give a combined **quality of life rating**.

Task 1: Quality of life

Make a copy of the chart below. Add more indicators of your own, and explain what they show about quality of life.

Indicator	What it shows about quality of life
Average earnings	A measure of wealth
Notified crimes	A measure of safety
Unemployment	Job opportunities/choices

Task 2: Quality of life in London

Figure 2.7 gives a range of indicators for quality of life across London (except in the City). London is divided into 33 boroughs (**Figure 2.8**). They are responsible for organising services such as education, housing, refuse collection, etc.

1 Working in small groups, select four indicators. Each member of the group must rank one indicator. Rank 1 is given to the borough with the 'best' figure, rank 2 to the 'second best', and so on. (Note that sometimes the highest figure will be the 'best' score and sometimes the lowest figure will be the 'best' score.) Complete a copy of **Figure 2.8** for each indicator, using the following key:

rank 1 to 8	*yellow*
rank 9 to 16	*orange*
rank 17 to 24	*brown*
rank 25 to 32	*red*.

2 Now add together the ranks for each of the four indicators. This will give you a combined **quality of life** score, or rating, for each borough. Put them in rank order and produce a map of the results, using the same key as before.

3 Compare your results with those of other groups in the class. Then write a description of your maps. Point out any patterns that you notice. Try to *explain* any patterns that you recognise.

▼ Figure 2.7

Quality of life in London.

Borough	Standard mortality rate	Weekly average earnings (male)	Notified crimes	Unemployment	Owner-occupied housing	% no car	5 or more GCSE A–C grades, 1995	Total	Rank
Barking & Dagenham	104.5	365.0	17,157	12.4	51.8	42.9	27.6		
Barnet	90.3	350.4	25,770	9.9	68.9	30.2	52.7		
Bexley	91.4	397.1	16,456	9.0	78.8	26.7	43.1		
Brent	97.3	381.2	30,192	15.9	57.7	43.4	35.1		
Bromley	87.6	340.4	25,356	7.6	77.9	25.6	47.4		
Camden	103.5	438.1	39,402	15.4	33.8	55.8	41.5		
Croydon	102.3	385.6	30,990	9.9	72.8	30.5	36.8		
Ealing	105.5	391.5	29,991	10.6	63.6	36.6	33.5		
Enfield	92.1	367.5	23,981	11.1	73.6	31.8	39.3		
Greenwich	104.8	351.4	30,494	14.2	47.1	43.6	28.3		
Hackney	117.3	332.2	33,270	21.8	26.9	61.7	23.9		
Hammersmith & Fulham	111.2	405.4	24,987	15.1	41.9	52.0	31.8		
Haringey	105.4	319.6	27,691	20.2	49.8	50.0	27.5		
Harrow	86.0	383.8	16,149	8.3	77.9	26.5	52.5		
Havering	98.4	348.9	19,091	8.3	78.8	26.0	42.1		
Hillingdon	93.1	430.3	22,346	7.5	73.2	24.4	37.8		
Hounslow	96.4	406.7	23,934	9.6	61.2	32.3	39.0		
Islington	108.7	433.6	29,888	19.5	26.7	59.9	17.4		
Kensington & Chelsea	96.2	393.0	29,506	12.0	39.9	50.5	36.2		
Kingston upon Thames	89.3	398.8	13,731	7.3	74.4	27.0	55.5		
Lambeth	111.0	421.5	47,584	19.8	36.2	55.4	23.2		
Lewisham	105.1	337.2	29,794	16.8	47.8	47.1	29.0		
Merton	90.2	348.2	19,019	10.3	70.5	33.8	39.0		
Newham	110.5	366.3	30,731	19.6	49.8	53.5	23.7		
Redbridge	94.8	353.2	21,195	10.1	78.2	29.9	45.1		
Richmond upon Thames	89.8	372.4	14,578	7.2	70.0	28.5	48.1		
Southwark	114.2	448.6	43,034	18.6	27.2	58.0	22.2		
Sutton	88.3	359.4	14,715	8.4	75.2	26.4	52.9		
Tower Hamlets	114.9	478.4	28,172	20.6	23.2	61.6	21.7		
Waltham Forest	98.5	338.2	22,720	14.7	61.5	42.9	32.7		
Wandsworth	109.3	357.9	35,506	12.8	53.6	44.0	30.0		
Westminster	96.3	481.3	67,739	11.5	35.1	57.7	28.8		

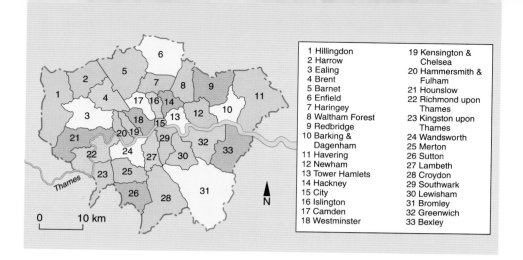

1 Hillingdon	19 Kensington & Chelsea
2 Harrow	20 Hammersmith & Fulham
3 Ealing	21 Hounslow
4 Brent	22 Richmond upon Thames
5 Barnet	23 Kingston upon Thames
6 Enfield	24 Wandsworth
7 Haringey	25 Merton
8 Waltham Forest	26 Sutton
9 Redbridge	27 Lambeth
10 Barking & Dagenham	28 Croydon
11 Havering	29 Southwark
12 Newham	30 Lewisham
13 Tower Hamlets	31 Bromley
14 Hackney	32 Greenwich
15 City	33 Bexley
16 Islington	
17 Camden	
18 Westminster	

◀ **Figure 2.8**
The London boroughs.

It should be clear from your maps that quality of life in outer London is better than the quality of life in inner London. This seems to be the case whichever indicators are used. The difference in quality of life seems to offer an explanation for the changing populations of inner and outer London. Inner London's population has been declining for some time. Although the figure for outer London has also been declining, it has been doing so at a slower rate. Population changes like these may have affected the population structure of these two areas – see Figure 2.9.

Bromley has a much older age profile. Many people choose to move out of inner London in later life. Why should they wish to do this?

▼ **Figure 2.9**
Population pyramids for Wandsworth (inner London) and Bromley (outer London).

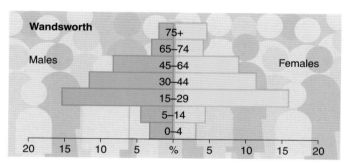

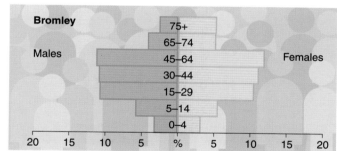

Task 3

Read in **Figure 2.10** about the opinions of two people living in different parts of London.

1 What does Alan like about his area? Why would he not want to live in central London?

2 What does Sally like about her area? Why would she not want to live in outer London?

▼ **Figure 2.10**
A difference of opinion.

Alan and Sally are both teachers in Tower Hamlets, east London. Alan lives in outer London, whilst Sally lives in Islington, inner London. They have both made decisions about where they wish to live.

Sally lives in a large house in Islington. She likes the house and the area. She has many friends who live locally. Sally often visits the theatre and eats out at restaurants quite often. She likes being close to these facilities and would not wish to live in the suburbs, as she would not have the access and choice she has at present.

Alan lives in the London borough of Bromley. He likes the rural atmosphere of the area. He enjoys the fields and wildlife around his home. It takes him about 40 minutes to get to work. His home is on a private estate, so it is quiet and there are few problems with traffic. Alan likes the local shops and rarely visits central London. He would not like to live in inner London because of the noise and the traffic.

Task 4: Quality of life within London

Pick **four** indicators and produce a quality of life map for Tower Hamlets. Use the following key:

rank 1 to 5   *yellow*
rank 6 to 10   *orange*
rank 11 to 15 *brown*
rank 16 to 19 *red.*

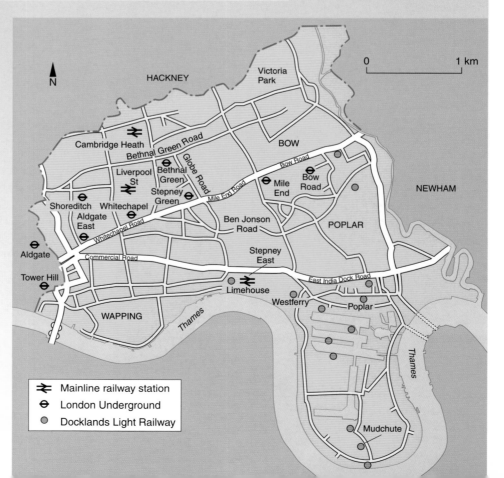

	% owner-occupied homes	% no car	% male unemployed	% with long-term illness	% more than 1.5 people per room
Blackwall	20.1	60.6	28.6	15.3	4.1
Bow	27.0	65.7	22.2	15.2	1.5
Bromley	14.7	67.9	27.6	13.3	3.7
East India	24.9	61.5	24.3	15.4	2.0
Grove	45.8	50.1	18.1	12.9	1.6
Holy Trinity	19.4	64.9	29.1	15.3	5.6
Lansbury	20.0	63.4	27.2	16.9	2.8
Limehouse	22.3	63.2	28.2	16.2	4.9
Millwall	33.9	45.8	20.1	12.4	1.9
Park	17.2	63.8	23.2	18.7	0.8
Redcoat	19.9	64.9	26.2	17.0	3.6
St Dunstan's	16.3	68.6	31.7	15.5	7.5
St James's	21.4	64.3	24.7	17.7	2.4
St Katharine's	30.4	54.6	24.1	12.3	6.6
St Mary's	20.6	68.7	24.6	13.6	6.8
St Peter's	25.0	65.3	26.4	13.6	5.1
Shadwell	22.0	58.1	26.2	12.9	7.8
Spitalfields	18.1	73.6	35.6	13.0	16.0
Weavers	18.0	66.8	28.8	13.9	5.2

Figure 2.11

◀ *Quality of life indicators for the borough of Tower Hamlets.*

▶ **Figure 2.12**

The London borough of Tower Hamlets.

◀ **Figure 2.13**
Grove (above) and Spitalfields (left), wards of Tower Hamlets borough in inner London.

◀ **Figure 2.14**
Hilldene ward in Havering, an outer London borough.

Your map shows that some wards have a much higher quality of life than others. The Grove ward consistently comes out well, whilst a ward like Spitalfields is always near the bottom. The Spitalfields area is on the edge of the City of London, the main commercial and business district of London. It is an area with a lot of **private rented housing**. It has a high turnover of people – many people who are newly arrived in London start off here and then move on when they find a more permanent place to live. Grove, on the other hand, is an area of **owner-occupied housing** overlooking Victoria Park. Its residents are settled and have well-paid jobs. It is interesting to compare Grove with wards in outer London boroughs. Havering and Croydon have higher overall ratings but the figures for the wards of Hilldene and Fielding tell a different story (Figure 2.15).

► **Figure 2.15**
Quality of life in wards of inner and outer London (percentage figures).

	Ward		
	Grove (Tower Hamlets)	**Hilldene** (Havering)	**Fielding** (Croydon)
Owner-occupied housing	45.8	42.0	34.0
Unemployment	18.1	17.0	21.8
No car	50.1	45.5	45.2
Long-term illness	12.9	18.5	10.6

Task 5

Which aspects of quality of life are better in Grove (inner London) than in Hilldene and Fielding (both outer London)?

Extension activity

Obtain census data for a city near you and attempt an analysis of the quality of life between the inner and outer areas. Census information is available in most public libraries, possibly in the form of a CD-ROM.

Summary

When considering quality of life it is important to remember that scale can hide differences between areas. We must also bear in mind which facilities people wish to be close to. This will change from person to person.

Urban structure

In this section we study five main ideas:

1 Towns contain a variety of different residential areas.

2 Geographers try to identify patterns in the layout of cities.

3 'Models' of urban structure (layout) can help us to understand why such patterns occur.

4 There are good reasons why real urban places do not conform to such models.

5 There have been important changes to housing provision in the UK.

Cities can often look similar. This is because they have similar functions. In the previous section we saw that quality of life tends to increase towards the edge of the city. If we examine housing or residential areas more closely it is possible to identify different types of houses. Four of the most common housing types in the UK are described here (Figure 2.16).

◀ **Figure 2.16**
One type of housing (see also next page).

Terraced houses
These are usually old houses built in the mid-19th century. A terrace means a long row of houses joined together. The houses are often small with just two bedrooms. They were originally built without inside toilets or bathrooms. Generally these have been added later. Small back gardens are common. There are no garages and so the streets are often full of parked cars.

Figure 2.16 (continued)
Different types of housing.

Semi-detached houses

This is when two houses are joined together. They usually have a small front garden and a large back garden. Many were built during the 1920s and 1930s when cities in the UK rapidly expanded their suburbs into the surrounding countryside. The houses are quite large, usually with three or four bedrooms.

Detached houses

A detached house stands on its own. It may be surrounded by a garden and often has a garage. Such houses are large with three, four or more bedrooms.

Flats

These may be low-rise flats with just two or three storeys or they may be high-rise buildings with up to 30 or 40 storeys. Flats are self-contained accommodation within a larger building. They do not have gardens although they are often surrounded by public open space.

The other important factor about housing in the UK is tenure. **Tenure** means the legal circumstances in which a person occupies a house. People may be **council tenants**, which means they rent their home from the local authority or council. They may be **private tenants**, which means they rent from a private landlord. Or they may own their home, or be buying it on a mortgage. This means they are **owner-occupiers**.

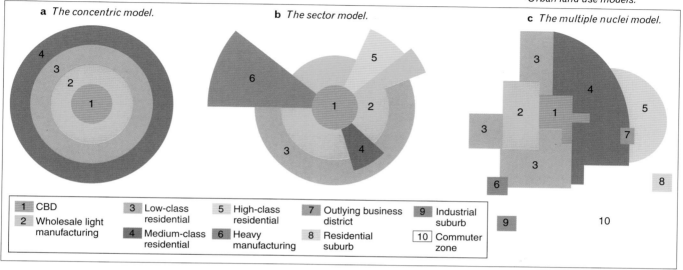

a *The concentric model.* b *The sector model.* c *The multiple nuclei model.*

| 1 | CBD | 3 | Low-class residential | 5 | High-class residential | 7 | Outlying business district | 9 | Industrial suburb |
| 2 | Wholesale light manufacturing | 4 | Medium-class residential | 6 | Heavy manufacturing | 8 | Residential suburb | 10 | Commuter zone |

These different housing types tend to occur in groups. Sociologists, economists and geographers have looked for reasons to explain this grouping (Figure 2.17). One idea, from a sociologist who lived in Chicago in the 1920s, was that towns grew outwards in a series of concentric rings (Figures 2.17a and 2.18). In the centre were shops and offices, in a space called the **central business district** or CBD (Figure 2.19). Shops and offices are located in the centre because it is the most accessible place. Around the CBD the land is in a **zone of transition**, because it may be bought for development. Buildings are often left empty until they are sold, and such areas can become very run down. Beyond this is a ring of industry and low-quality housing. This is the zone of cheap accommodation where new migrants to the city gather in search of a place to live and work. The quality of housing then increases outwards through the various rings, as people with a good income are attracted to life in the suburbs.

▼ **Figure 2.18**
Cross-section of a concentric zone model.

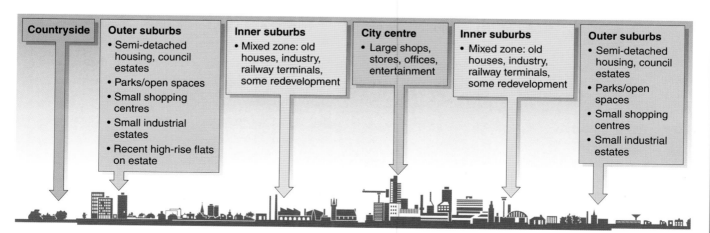

Countryside	Outer suburbs	Inner suburbs	City centre	Inner suburbs	Outer suburbs
	• Semi-detached housing, council estates • Parks/open spaces • Small shopping centres • Small industrial estates • Recent high-rise flats on estate	• Mixed zone: old houses, industry, railway terminals, some redevelopment	• Large shops, stores, offices, entertainment	• Mixed zone: old houses, industry, railway terminals, some redevelopment	• Semi-detached housing, council estates • Parks/open spaces • Small shopping centres • Small industrial estates

▶ **Figure 2.19**
*Part of the central business
district of Birmingham.*

Another model was produced by an economist (Figure 2.17b). In the 1940s, he looked at housing and rents in 142 North American cities. He found that land uses often developed in **sectors** radiating outwards from the CBD. High-quality housing tended to occupy pleasant locations in the city. Industry often developed along roads and railways. Low-rent housing tended to be squeezed in, near to noisy or dirty industrial locations. A third North American model suggested that towns did not just develop one centre but that other points in the city can become commercially important because they also have good **accessibility** (Figure 2.17c). For instance, a small shopping centre may build up around a new railway station. This idea is known as the **multiple nuclei model**.

These models are not intended to be exact fits for all cities. They simplify reality in order to help us to identify *patterns* that result from different *processes*. It is possible to examine the land use in real towns and cities and use the models to suggest reasons for the land use pattern. On the following pages we use Swindon as an example.

Activities

1 Make a copy of the three land use models.

2 Describe the main points of the three models, and explain why they are different.

Swindon: an example of urban structure

Background

Swindon is located approximately halfway between London and Bristol (Figure 2.20). It lies very close to the M4 motorway and the London–Bristol railway line. The early growth of Swindon owes much to the railway industry. It became a centre for repairing trains in the late 19th century. Those works are now closed. However, the town is still an important industrial centre. Many factories have been attracted to the town in the last 20 years because Swindon's position on the motorway network makes it very accessible. This growth in industry has meant that many new houses have been built. Swindon increased its population by over 20,000 between 1971 and 1991.

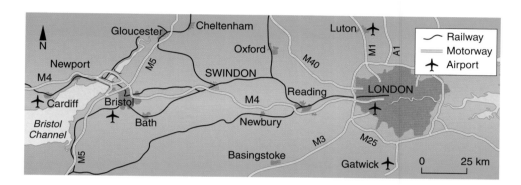

◀ **Figure 2.20**
The locality of Swindon.

▼ **Figure 2.21**
Part of the 1:50 000 OS map of the Swindon area.

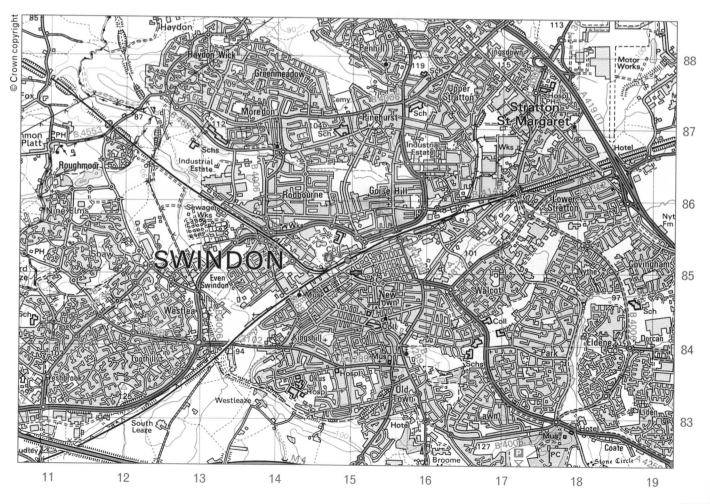

Housing

All the housing types described on pages 33–34 can be found in Swindon. Figure 2.21 shows part of the 1:50 000 OS map of Swindon, while some of the different housing areas and parts of the 1:25 000 OS map can be seen in Figure 2.22. Below the photographs is a selection of information from the 1991 census.

Toothill

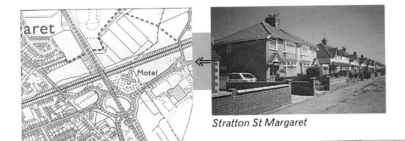

Map extracts © Crown copyright

Stratton St Margaret

Park

Central

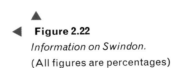

	Wards			
	Toothill	**Stratton St Margaret**	**Central**	**Park**
Tenure				
Owner-occupied	81	90	67	39
Private rented	8	6	16	3
Council rented	11	4	17	58
No car	16	16	46	48
Socio-economic status (these figures do not necessarily add up to 100%)				
Professional	9	6	3	0
Managerial & technical	36	30	22	15
Skilled manual	21	24	32	35
Skilled non-manual	16	17	16	13
Unskilled	2	3	6	9
Age/Sex				
Male 0–4	5.4	3.3	3.5	4.7
5–14	7.6	6.0	3.6	6.9
15–29	14.4	11.7	16.9	11.8
30–44	14.7	11.2	10.2	8.6
45–64	5.8	12.6	9.6	10.8
65–74	1.5	3.4	7.5	4.2
75+	0.8	1.8	2.7	1.5
Age/Sex				
Female 0–4	4.8	3.1	2.9	4.1
5–14	7.5	5.3	3.5	6.4
15–29	15.4	11.5	15.1	11.8
30–44	13.4	10.7	7.3	9.2
45–64	5.6	12.3	8.2	12.3
65–74	1.9	3.9	4.7	4.7
75+	1.2	3.3	4.3	2.8

▲

◀ **Figure 2.22**

Information on Swindon.

(All figures are percentages)

Activity

Use the information from **Figures 2.21** and **2.22** to complete the following chart.

Ward	Distance from town centre	Type of houses	Tenure	Age structure	Socio-economic groups	Car ownership
Central						
Park						
Stratton						
Toothill						

Use the information in your table to write a paragraph comparing Stratton and Central wards. Your paragraph should include details of location, population, house type and the environment.

Swindon and land use models

Figure 2.23 is a land use map of Swindon. Housing areas have been divided into three categories:

Category 1
Mainly detached and semi-detached houses – large numbers of owner-occupiers.

Category 2
Mainly terraced houses and flats – large numbers of private and council tenants.

Category 3
Mixed housing.

◀ **Figure 2.23**
Land use in Swindon.

Activities

1 Which of the three models shown on page 35 does Swindon most resemble?

2 In what ways does Swindon's land use pattern differ from the model you have chosen?

Why does Swindon differ from the models?

The multiple nuclei model concentrated on urban growth and accessibility, and it is not surprising that Swindon resembles this model most. The other models do not really suit cities in the UK. For example, it is difficult to study a UK city properly without thinking about housing tenure. In the USA all housing is either privately owned or privately rented, but from 1920 large areas of new building in UK cities were in the form of council housing. During the 1980s much of that changed. Council tenants were given the right to buy their properties, and many people did so. Look at the figures for home ownership in Swindon for 1981 and 1991 (Figure 2.24).

Ward	1981	1991
Blunsdon	56.3	78.7
Central	73.0	67.1
Chiseldon	59.9	72.3
Covingham	93.6	94.9
Dorcan	57.1	73.4
Eastcott	82.7	81.2
Freshbrook	–	78.4
Gorse Hill	62.7	66.3
Haydon Wick	–	88.9
Highworth	68.9	73.9
Lawns	87.9	87.1
Moredon	56.4	62.2
Park	7.8	39.1
Ridgeway	57.4	74.4
St Philip	61.6	73.4
Stratton St Margaret	90.3	90.1
Toothill	–	80.4
Walcot	48.6	59.5
Western	83.1	82.6
Whitworth	14.6	34.4
Wroughton	66.8	73.3

▲ **Figure 2.24**
Home ownership in Swindon, 1981 and 1991 (percentage figures).

Areas with already high levels of home ownership showed little increase or even a slight decrease. However, areas with previously low levels of ownership such as Park and Whitworth saw large increases.

Throughout the 1980s home ownership increased across the country and house prices rose steeply. However, during the 1990s many people found it difficult to keep up with payments for their homes (Figure 2.25). Houses have become cheaper to buy in the 1990s, but this has caused some new home owners to face the problem of negative equity: they cannot sell their house because it is worth less than the money they borrowed (their mortgage) to buy it in the first place.

▶ **Figure 2.25**
From The Guardian,
27 July 1995

Home loan evictions increase as prices drop and lenders run out of patience

Home repossessions have risen for the first time in four years with the threat of more to come.
One of Britain's leading mortgage lenders warned yesterday there was little prospect of house prices increasing this side of a general election.
The Council of Mortgage

Lenders highlighted the threat of a renewed decline in Britain's already depressed housing market with the release of figures showing that 25,200 homes were taken into possession in the first half of this year. It blamed the Government for adding to the problem of negative equity by making benefit rules tougher.

Activities

1 How many homes were taken into possession in the first half of 1995?

2 What is *negative equity*?

3 How do you think increasing home ownership might change an area?

4 How are the urban land use models useful?

Summary

As we have seen with Swindon, towns do not 'fit' the models exactly. But models do provide a framework within which cities can be compared. They also help us to focus on the main reasons in the past for the development of a particular city.

People and services

In this section we consider four key ideas:

1 People require a variety of services to meet their daily needs.

2 There is a hierarchy in the provision of services – larger cities have more services to offer than smaller ones.

3 People's ability to use services varies, and depends on a number of factors.

4 Services are provided by public bodies such as the local authority, and private companies. They provide services for different reasons.

Wherever people live they have to be able to buy food and clothes. Schools are built to educate children, and hospitals to serve people's health needs. People must be able to get from place to place along transport routes.

The larger the settlement is, the more services it can provide because it has a larger threshold population. For a shop to be successful it needs a certain **threshold population** to provide enough customers. This means there may only be enough people in a small village to support one shop, but a town will be able to support many shops. The way thresholds work results in the **settlement hierarchy** (Figure 2.26). Settlements at the top of the hierarchy have services with a large threshold and **range**.

The relationship between settlement size and the supply of services is not always simple. For example, services can be organised in different ways. Some services are offered by private companies and some by local and central government. Private companies run services, for example shops, because the owner feels that it is possible to make a profit by providing people with the things they need. Local and central government services are provided to meet the needs of local people. They are not run primarily as businesses to make a profit, but are paid for by money collected from local and national taxes. Since 1980 many of the services provided by local councils have been transferred to private companies. This has meant a real change in the way some local services are organised, as businesses. Examples of local services which have been switched from public to private provision include bus services and household refuse collection. Nationally, too, some services have passed into private hands, such as water supply, gas and electricity, as well as the railways.

▼ **Figure 2.26**
Hierarchy of settlements.

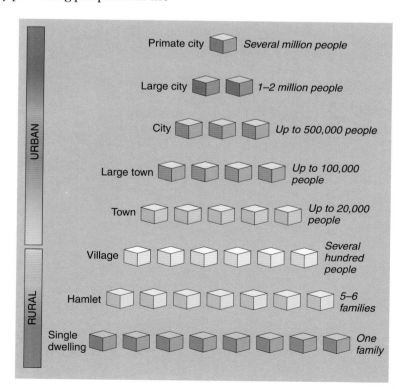

People disagree about whether this is a good idea. Some feel that the old public services wasted money and were inefficient. Others feel that private companies only run things to make a profit, and therefore cut out services that are expensive or difficult to run, for example bus routes to isolated villages.

Activities

1 a Make a copy of **Figure 2.26**.

  b For each level of settlement name a place that you know.

2 a Name a service in your area that has switched from being a public operation to being a private operation.

  b Do you think this service has improved or declined since the change? You should ask some adults to help you answer this question.

Access to services

The number of services provided in an area is dependent upon the population. As population changes in an area then so does the number of services provided. Rural North Yorkshire provides us with a good example of this.

Upper Wharfedale is a scenic valley in the Yorkshire Dales National Park. Changes in population structure (see Unit 1) and employment opportunities have altered the characteristics of the villages dotted along the valley. Services that once existed in the local villages seem to be disappearing.

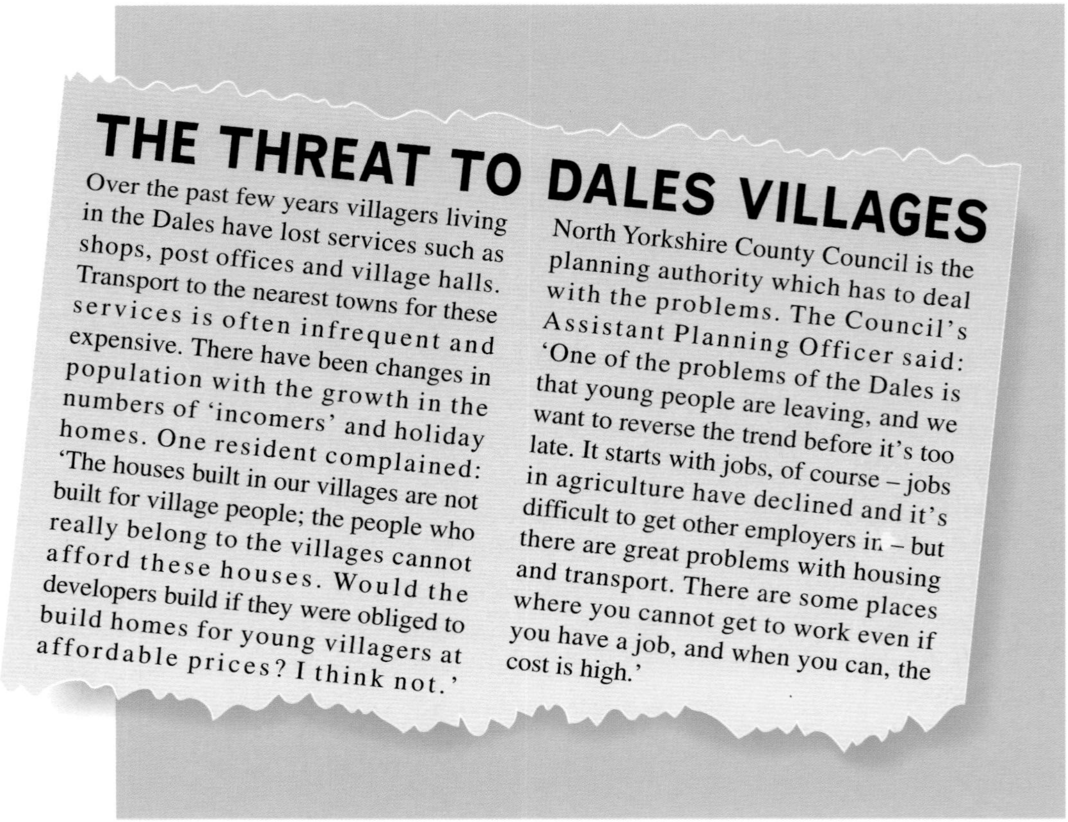

▶ **Figure 2.27**
A changing lifestyle.

THE THREAT TO DALES VILLAGES

Over the past few years villagers living in the Dales have lost services such as shops, post offices and village halls. Transport to the nearest towns for these services is often infrequent and expensive. There have been changes in population with the growth in the numbers of 'incomers' and holiday homes. One resident complained: 'The houses built in our villages are not built for village people; the people who really belong to the villages cannot afford these houses. Would the developers build if they were obliged to build homes for young villagers at affordable prices? I think not.'

North Yorkshire County Council is the planning authority which has to deal with the problems. The Council's Assistant Planning Officer said: 'One of the problems of the Dales is that young people are leaving, and we want to reverse the trend before it's too late. It starts with jobs, of course – jobs in agriculture have declined and it's difficult to get other employers in – but there are great problems with housing and transport. There are some places where you cannot get to work even if you have a job, and when you can, the cost is high.'

Figure 2.28
Upper Wharfedale – part of the
1: 50 000 OS map sheet 98
© Crown copyright

Services	Grassington	Conistone	Kilnsey	Kettlewell	Starbotton
Post office	1	–	–	1	1
Public house	3	–	1	3	1
Church	2	1	–	1	–
School	1	–	–	–	–
Café/restaurant	6	–	–	2	–
Village hall	1	–	–	1	–
Food shop	9	–	–	3	–
Non-food shop	17	–	–	1	–
Garage/petrol	1	–	–	1	–
Hotel/bed & breakfast	3	1	–	4	2
Total services	44	2	1	17	4

Source: Data collected by students at Acland Burghley School

Ages	% male	% female	Total %
0–4	2	1	3
5–9	2	2	4
10–14	2	3	5
15–19	2	3	5
20–24	2	3	5
25–29	3	2	5
30–34	1	2	3
35–39	2	4	6
40–44	4	3	7
45–49	3	3	6
50–54	2	4	6
55–59	3	4	7
60–64	4	4	8
65–69	4	5	9
70–74	3	4	7
75–79	3	3	6
80–84	1	4	5
85–89	0	3	3
90 and over	0	0	0

a *Population structure of Grassington.*

▼ **Figure 2.30**   *Population and population structure in selected Dales villages.*

	1931	1951	1961	1971	1981	1991
Grassington	1,076	1,151	1,131	1,330	1,215	1,102
Conistone & Kilnsey	138	127	103	111	115	113
Kettlewell & Starbotton	330	304	290	333	310	297

b *Population totals, 1931–91.*

Activities

1 a How far are the villages of Starbotton and Arncliffe from Grassington?

b Give a six-figure grid reference for the centre of Kettlewell.

2 Which settlement has most services and which has the least?

3 Name three problems identified in the newspaper article in **Figure 2.27**.

4 Which village or pair of villages had the largest population decline between 1931 and 1991 (**Figure 2.30b**)?

5 A settlement hierarchy is when the settlements in an area are arranged in levels of 'importance' – services with a greater threshold and range are located in fewer, larger settlements. Work with a partner or a small group for this activity.

a Decide which information on these pages you are going to use to help you decide how important each settlement in Wharfedale is.

b Choose a method to display your information so that it is easy to spot which settlements are more important and which are less important. Some ideas include pie charts, bar charts and graphs to show the relationships (or correlation) between two variables.

c Write a description summarising what your display techniques show.

d Write a final list of settlements in order of importance according to your analysis.

Figure 2.31
Conistone village.

Figure 2.32
Grassington.

Extension activity

6 Is there any spatial pattern to your settlement hierarchy for Upper Wharfedale? For example, do settlements lower in the hierarchy tend to be concentrated in one part of the valley? Explain your answer.

7 Which settlements in the valley do you think are most likely to decline in the future, and how will this decline take place?

Many of the services for the people of Wharfedale are not provided by the settlements in the valley. Where would they buy a new carpet or visit the cinema? Such a level of service is only possible in a larger settlement. People in the valley have to travel to large towns such as Lancaster, Ripon or York.

Just as services are changing in Wharfedale they are also changing in towns and cities. One recent trend in the provision of shops is the growth of out-of-town shopping malls. These are located on the edge of urban places at very accessible locations. The malls have large free car parks, and as more and more people shop by car and city centres have become congested, they have grown in popularity. People buy in bulk and shop at a time convenient to them. This has meant that some shops in city centres have closed down.

◀ **Figure 2.33**
Some views on York.

Empty Shops Blow for York

Many shops in the heart of York still remain empty despite a record number of tourists, a survey by the *Yorkshire Evening Press* reveals today. The number of empty shops in 18 main streets within the city walls is now 72 – a slight decline from 76 exactly a year ago.

Worst-affected streets remain Walmgate and Micklegate, with 12 and 10 shopfronts respectively.

From the Yorkshire Evening Press, August 1993

Store Wars Flare

Sainsbury's plans for a 68,000 sq.ft superstore represent an attempt to hit back at arch-rival Tesco. Tesco is on course to open its second superstore in York later this year after the runaway success of its Clifton Moor store, opened two years ago. Sainsbury said that its new store would create 350 jobs. Of these about two-thirds would be part-time.

A report to planners at Selby District Council forecasts: "There would only be minimal impact upon the viability of the city centre and nearby suburban local centres." The two developments together would provide 4,000 parking spaces.

From the Yorkshire Evening Post, April 1990

Megastore Sparks Ghost Town Fears

A huge discount store which council planners fear could threaten the future of York city centre is getting ready to open at Clifton Moor.

York and Ryedale councils lost a battle to stop the Matalan store, which they believe could turn York into a ghost town ringed with out-of-town superstores.

Dave Curtis, development manager for York City Council, stressed that the Council would have to re-double its efforts to ensure the city centre remained a lively and viable shopping centre. He said: "We are obviously concerned that this is another straw on the camel's back. I don't know when it's going to break but without doubt this store together with the others will have an impact on the city centre shopping."

From the Yorkshire Evening Post, February 1993

A Paradise for Shoppers

"York has a well-managed shopping heart with a co-ordinated approach to a variety of initiatives including footstreets, shoppers' car parking, park-and-ride and access for disabled people."

From the Yorkshire Evening Press, November 1992

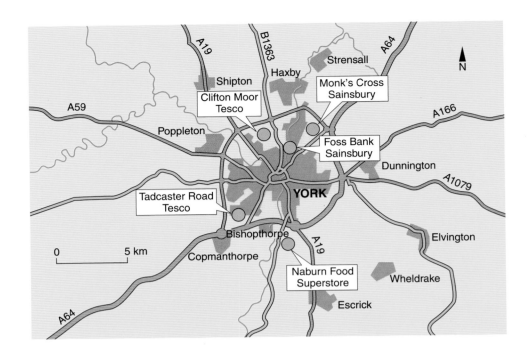

Activities

1 Which groups of people do you think would suffer most from the decline of the high street shops?

2 Draft a letter to the *Yorkshire Evening Post* giving your opinion of the out-of-town shopping centres and their effects on the city.

Not all people use services in the same way. The needs of a young family, for example, are different from those of a retired couple without children. This means they make use of a different selection of services.

People's ability to use the services in a settlement depends on a variety of factors. Those with a high disposable income have a wide choice. Those who are able to travel easily (have the greatest **mobility**) also have a choice of services, as do those with most leisure time. The people who have the greatest choice, or command, of services are those with a combination of all of these factors.

Activities

1 Make a copy of this chart. Rank the services in the order you think each person or group would find most essential. Give the most essential service rank 1, the second most essential rank 2, and so on.

Service	Young family	Single person, mid-20s	Retired person
• Primary school			
• Post office			
• Taxi firm			
• Youth club			
• Supermarket			
• Corner shop			
• Theatre			
• Public house			
• Garage			
• Health and fitness club			
• Shopping mall			

2 a Study the graphs below. They show the distances travelled by swimmers and squash players to a large sports centre.

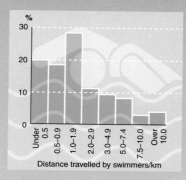

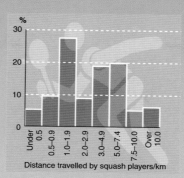

Distance travelled by swimmers/km

Distance travelled by squash players/km

(i) What percentage of swimmers travelled less than 2 km to use the sports centre?

(ii) What percentage of squash players travelled less than 7.5 km to use the sports centre?

b Study Resource A below. The graphs show the age, sex and socio-economic group of swimmers and squash players.

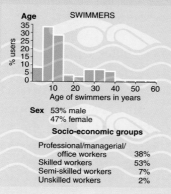

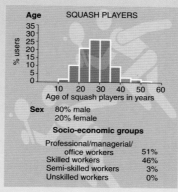

Resource A

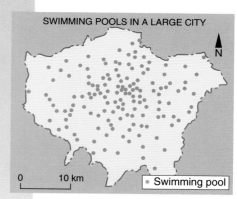

Resource B

(i) Describe the age distribution of
  • swimmers
  • squash players.

(ii) How does the information in Resource A help to explain the differences in the distance people travel to swim and play squash, in terms of age, sex and socio-economic group?

c Study Resource B. It shows the distribution of public swimming pools in a large city.

(i) Describe the distribution of public swimming pools.

(ii) How would you expect the distribution of squash courts to be different from the distribution of swimming pools? Explain your answer.

d Choose another service or amenity (other than swimming pools or squash courts). Describe and account for its distribution or location in a city, and show why it is not equally accessible to all members of the community. Use a sketch-map if you wish.

MEG 1992

The car and the city

There are now half a billion (500 million) cars on the world's roads. The global vehicle population is growing at the massive rate of 19 million a year. By the middle of the next century, car fumes are expected to be the largest single contributor to global warming.

This section looks at the North American city of Los Angeles, to see how the car has created not only serious environmental problems, but also social divisions between those who can afford to get around by car and those who cannot. In contrast, the Brazilian city of Curitiba has invested in a public transport system which means that even those who cannot afford a car can travel cheaply and efficiently to school and work, avoiding the worst of the social and environmental problems of a city dominated by the car.

Los Angeles – a city divided by the car?

Los Angeles appears to be an extremely convenient city. It has hundreds of kilometres of 'freeways' criss-crossing the city and its suburbs. Cars in Los Angeles on average move three times faster than in European cities like London where narrow streets and traffic lights restrict the flow.

However, this impression of speed hides a major problem: Los Angeles residents also have to travel three times as far. In European cities population densities are higher than in Los Angeles, which has less than a tenth of London's population density. Speed is not much of an advantage when the additional distance you have to travel soaks up your time. The extracts in Figure 2.36 point out other problems, too.

◀ **Figure 2.35**
Freeways in Los Angeles.

▼ **Figure 2.36**
The problems of moving people around Los Angeles.

Los Angeles has a transport system that has deepened social divides. Although the city has the second largest bus fleet in the USA, only 3% of journeys are made by bus. Most of the bus services are concentrated in the inner-city areas where population densities are highest and the city's poorest people live. For most of these poor, however, the city bus service is too expensive to use. If you live in the suburbs bus services are rare. Getting to school, going to the bank or going shopping all involve car journeys. People have to drive because things are so spread out, but if you can't afford a car, getting around becomes very difficult. There is a big social division in Los Angeles between the people who can afford a car and live in the suburbs, and those who can't and live in the inner city.

The car also damages people's health. The city is famous for its photochemical "smog", a kind of airborne soup made of car fumes warmed by the sun. Cars have also changed what the city looks like. The older, more historic parts of the inner city are being pulled apart to make more room for the car. Every mile of motorway takes up 10 hectares of land. But motorways are in fact a very inefficient way of carrying people. A standard six-lane motorway can carry 120,000 passengers a day. In comparison, a two-track railway, which takes up only one-sixth of the space of a motorway, can carry 200,000 people.

Figure 2.37
Downtown Los Angeles:
a *with a build-up of smog, and*
b *on a clear day.*

Rather than spend millions of dollars on a road-building programme which has no effect on solving the problems caused by the motor car, the Los Angeles city authorities may have done well to look at the example of Curitiba, a Brazilian city, for solutions.

Curitiba

Curitiba is the capital city of Brazil's southern state of Parana. In 1971 it had a population of 500,000, and in the mid-1990s 1.6 million. Such massive urban growth could have caused an urban transport disaster, but instead Curitiba has won international awards for its urban planning.

In Curitiba one in five people own a car. Yet compared with other Brazilian cities, these people use 25 per cent less petrol. This saving in fuel is linked to the success of the city's **Integrated Transport System**. Based on bus networks and built upon existing roads, the system has been designed to serve all sections of the community.

There are four main bus lines. Express (red) buses use specially designated bus lanes to speed up to 150 passengers at a time into the city centre. Direct (grey) buses follow the same routes but stop more. The inter-neighbourhood buses (green) are designed for people who want to travel around the city, and follow concentric routes. The feeder buses (yellow) pick up people on local routes and feed into the faster network.

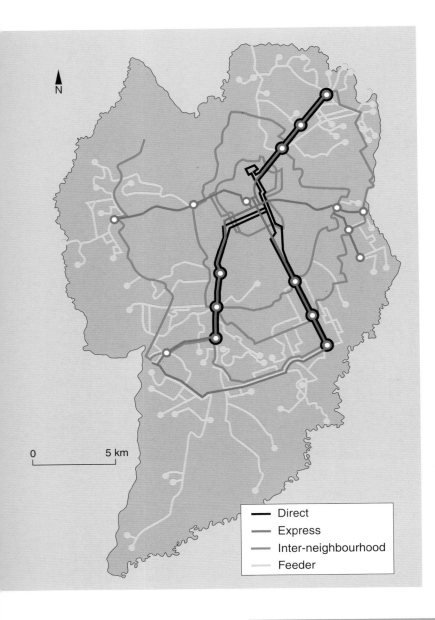

Key:
- Direct
- Express
- Inter-neighbourhood
- Feeder

0   5 km

In the mid-1970s around 25,000 people used the city's buses each day. In the 1990s the Integrated Transport System enables 1.3 million journeys to be made, daily.

Passengers are positively encouraged. For example, bus stops, every 400 metres, are equipped with telephones, newspaper kiosks and post office facilities. There are 20 purpose-built bus terminals which have become important meeting points – these are the city's multiple nuclei (see Figure 2.17c).

The success of the plan is immediately clear to the visitor. Traffic flows freely along wide tree-shaded avenues. There are few traffic jams and the air is noticeably free of traffic fumes. The scheme has been so successful because traffic management has been linked to improving social conditions. Curitiba has shown that an efficient city transport system can give all sections of its community access to services and improve their quality of life. Indeed, Curitiba's successful transport planning is the envy of many wealthier nations.

◀ **Fig 2.38**
Curitiba's Integrated Transport System.

Activities

1 Select five facts which you think show there is a 'global' crisis caused by the motor car.

2 What social, environmental and economic problems does Los Angeles face because of its traffic?

3 Imagine you are the Mayor of Curitiba and have received a letter from the Mayor of Los Angeles, which sets out what the Los Angeles transport system is like and the problems associated with it. Reply with information and advice on how to solve the problems. Your reply should cover the following:

• The problems Curitiba faced with traffic and poverty.

• A description of the scheme and its social, environmental and economic advantages.

• A summary of the reasons why you think the scheme has been a success.

• Your recommendations as to what could be done in Los Angeles.

Changing cities: case study of Paris

We have seen that settlements have to meet people's everyday needs. Over time the things that people want change, and cities also must change. Some changes have lasting effects on cities. Other changes cater for new fashions and may not last. Change in a city is sometimes organised through a plan. Often it is not, and change is then haphazard or unplanned. Paris is one example of a major European city that has changed in all of these ways.

Until 1850, although its population had been increasing, the area occupied by the city had not. Paris was contained within a fortified wall. However, this medieval city was not able to meet the needs of its 19th-century population. The population continued to rise, houses were overcrowded and conditions were poor.

▲ **Figure 2.39**
Satellite image of Paris.

▼ **Figure 2.40**
Paris.

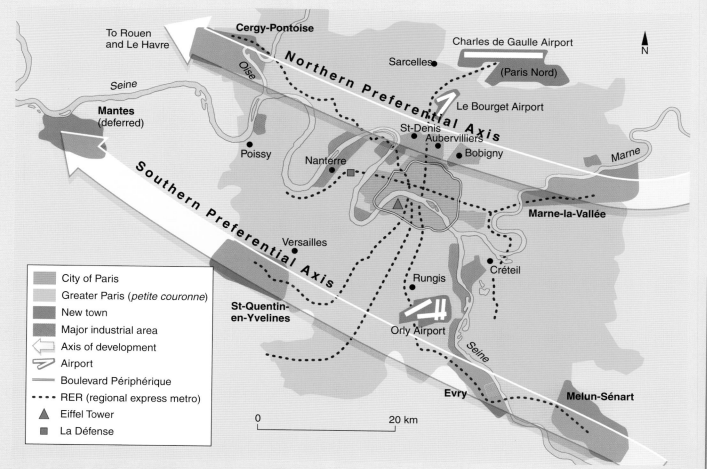

Legend:
- City of Paris
- Greater Paris (*petite couronne*)
- New town
- Major industrial area
- Axis of development
- Airport
- Boulevard Périphérique
- RER (regional express metro)
- ▲ Eiffel Tower
- La Défense

0 — 20 km

▼ **Figure 2.41**
The Place d'Etoile.

In 1852 Napoleon III, the ruler of France, appointed Baron Haussman to lead a team that was to plan the modernisation of Paris. Haussman replaced a run-down area of the city with streets and buildings that remain today . This example of a planned change is centred around the Place d'Etoile.

To meet the growing demand for homes, land around the city was sold for building. Builders gambled on being able to sell the houses that they built. They were not disappointed. Many Parisians wished to move out of the crowded inner city to a detached house with a garden. Between 1918 and 1939, 80,000 homes were added to the suburbs of Paris. In 1950 the diameter of Paris was 10 kilometres, but by the 1980s it had stretched to 40 kilometres. Unfortunately for the residents, much of this development was unplanned and they were not always provided with adequate services such as shops and transport. At the same time, more and more people were moving to Paris. Some came from the countryside, some from other countries. They were mostly economic migrants looking for work. Within the city, tower blocks began to appear to help with the housing crisis. Once again the services needed by residents were not always provided. The statistics in Figure 2.42 show the changing population for the three areas of Paris – the central area, the inner suburbs known as the *petite couronne*, and the outer suburbs known as the *grande couronne*.

By the 1960s it was felt that an overall plan for Paris and the surrounding area

	Population		Percentage change
	1975	**1990**	
Paris	2,299,800	2,152,400	−6.8
Hauts de Seine	1,438,900	1,391,700	−3.4
Seine St-Denis	1,322,100	1,381,200	4.5
Val de Marne	1,215,700	1,215,500	0
Petite couronne (total)	3,976,700	3,998,400	0.5
Seine et Marne	755,800	1,078,200	42.6
Yvelines	1,082,300	1,307,100	20.8
Essonne	923,100	1,084,800	17.5
Val d'Oise	840,900	1,049,600	24.8
Grande couronne (total)	3,602,100	4,519,700	25.5

▲ **Figure 2.42**
The changing population of Paris.

▼ **Figure 2.43**
Some aspects of Paris.

a Seine St-Denis

b *La Défense*

c *Marne-la-Vallée*

d *Le Marais*

was needed. The Schéma Directeur was established in 1965. It identified several problems, or needs:

* to preserve the historic identity of the city
* to limit the outward growth of the suburbs
* to provide employment, shopping and transport facilities in the suburbs
* to link the inner city and the suburbs
* to provide homes with adequate facilities in the central area
* to provide new homes for the still increasing population.

The following are examples of how these needs were met:

* La Défense to the west of Paris (Figure 2.40) is the largest office development in Europe. It is a centre for employment and shopping with 65,000 jobs and 100,000 square metres of shops.

* The Schéma Directeur decided that within the *petite couronne* there should be nine centres where expansion should be encouraged (see the black dots on Figure 2.44). It was hoped that growth in these planned centres would prevent further suburban sprawl.

* A rapid rail system, the RER, was built to connect the suburbs to the inner city.

* Six new towns were developed around Paris linked by the RER. These have grown rapidly since the mid-1980s. St-Quentin-en-Yvelines, for example, has attracted a population of 75,000 people and is growing by about 10 per cent a year. Five hundred businesses have been established, providing employment for the residents.

* Grants for bathrooms and toilets were provided for the older properties in the central area. Money was also available to replace doors and windows, add bathrooms and repair roofs. Other areas were redeveloped on a large scale, and run-down areas of factories and housing were replaced by high-rise flats.

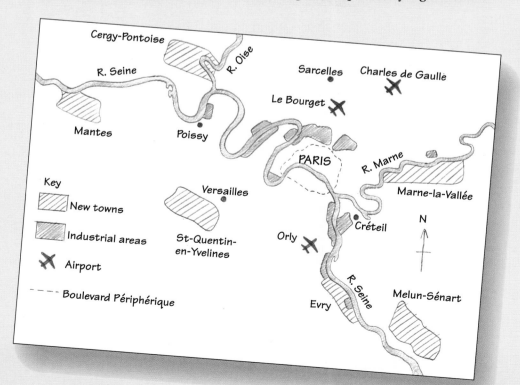

Figure 2.44
Sketch map of Paris.

* An area close to the River Seine called Le Marais was fashionable in the 17th century. It was an area of large mansions and well-laid-out squares. It had fallen into decline but now the area is being restored and there are many museums and galleries here.

The plan has been modified since the mid-1960s to take account of other changes, for instance:

* the **growth rate** of Paris is now declining

* there has been a loss of open space in and around the city

* more roads seem to have led to more traffic congestion.

The city also has to respond to changes in people's lifestyles. For instance:

• People have a growing concern for the environment.

• The use of computers may see a rise in the number of people working from home.

• The Channel Tunnel and Disneyland Paris will probably bring an increase in the number of tourists to the city.

Changes never stop, therefore, and it is sometimes difficult to predict what effect changes will have.

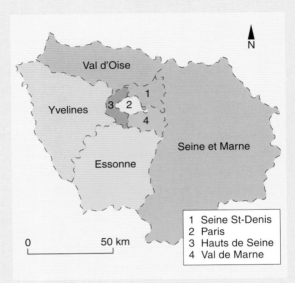

▼ **Figure 2.45**
Petite couronne.

1	Seine St-Denis
2	Paris
3	Hauts de Seine
4	Val de Marne

Activities

1 Analyse the case study of Paris. Give an example of:

   a planned change

   b haphazard change

   c a change that reflects a long-term trend

   d a change that reflects a fashion.

   If you have made a study of a British city, particularly London, it would be interesting to add to your analysis of Paris a *commentary* making comparisons between the two cities.

2 Using **Figures 2.39** and **2.40**, draw a sketch-map to show the main features of the area. You should try to draw a map that you could reproduce quickly from memory in an exam. **Figure 2.44** shows you how to start. Your map should be simple, but include important information such as:

   a the River Seine

   b the boundary of central Paris

   c the boundary of the suburbs

   d the RER lines

   e the new towns.

3 Use the information in **Figure 2.42** to complete a copy of **Figure 2.45**. Divide the figures into three or four groups. Use a different colour on the map for each group. Write a description of your finished map.

4 Use the information on pages 51–54 to complete the following chart.

Urban planning in Paris

Problem	Solution	Named example	Photograph
Preserving historic identity			
Limiting suburbs			
Providing services for suburbs			
Linking suburbs and inner city			
Improving housing in inner city			
Providing new homes			

5 **a** From your knowledge of urban geography, and referring to the case studies in this unit, what do you consider are the *likely* changes in European cities in the next 20 years?

   b What changes would you *hope for* in the next 20 years? Why?

Cities in the South

In 1960 there were only six cities in the world with a population of 5 million people or more. By 1980 there were 25 such cities. By the year 2000 there will be at least 60. More significant, it is expected that 45 of them will be in the South, the economically developing world. In this section we look at cities in the developing world. Cairo, the capital of Egypt is used as the main example to help us examine three common features of developing world cities:

* growth

* dominance of the largest city (the 'primate city')

* shortage of services.

Egypt – background information

Egypt has a population of about 58 million people. The country covers an area of just under 1 million square kilometres. However, only 4 per cent of the land is usable, and the rest is desert. This means that population density in the Nile Valley can be over 1,000 people per square kilometre. Temperatures in Cairo vary from 43 °C in the summer to 18 °C in the winter. Egypt depends on the River Nile for nearly all its water needs.

Agriculture remains the most important activity, employing over 45 per cent of the labour force and contributing 17 per cent of the country's exports. The main cash crop is cotton. Egypt also has considerable reserves of oil and gas which provide about 60 per cent of export earnings.

▲ **Figure 2.46**
Egypt.

Figure 2.47
Aspects of Cairo.

Rapid growth

Just as cities like London and Paris grew rapidly and expanded through the 19th and early 20th centuries, cities like São Paulo, Karachi and Cairo have shown rapid growth in the second half of the 20th century (Figure 2.48).

▶ **Figure 2.48**
The population of Cairo, 1930–90.

1930	1950	1960	1976	1980	1990
1.5 million	3 million	4.5 million	7 million	9 million	13 million

Cairo's population is growing rapidly for two reasons. First, there is natural increase of population (Figure 2.49).

Although the birth rate declined sharply between the 1950s and the 1970s, so did the death rate, which was already quite low. This meant that in the 1970s the population rose by 3 per cent a year. It has now slowed to just over 2 per cent. This means that the population of Egypt as a whole grows by over 1 million people a year.

▼ **Figure 2.49**
Cairo: natural population increase.

	1950s	1970s	1980s
Birth rate per 1,000	45.2	36.7	34.0
Death rate per 1,000	17.8	13.7	9.0

Not only does Cairo have to cope with a large annual natural increase, but the population pressure in Egypt as a whole makes Cairo a focus for migrants. People are leaving the countryside to search for work, and they hope for a better quality of life in the city.

Dominance of the largest city

One common feature of countries in the developing world is that one city begins to dominate all the others. Where a country's largest city is more than twice the size of the next largest city we can say that the country has a **primate city**. In Egypt, Cairo is six times larger than Alexandria, the country's second largest city.

A primate city can have several effects. It means that many people in the country see it as the *only* urban centre, so it attracts more and more people. This leads to constant demands for more houses and better transport facilities. Investment by the government and by private companies tends to be centred on the city and this makes it more difficult to develop the other regions of the country.

Egypt's answer

The Egyptian government has tried to counter this trend by encouraging the growth of cities such as Alexandria, Suez and Port Said. For example, it has established free trade zones in these cities as a means of attracting industry: companies are offered incentives, such as lower taxes, for several years. The government hopes that new jobs in these three cities will attract people who might otherwise have migrated to Cairo.

The government has also encouraged people to stay in the countryside. Four hundred new villages have been created and local factories developed to process farm products. There is also a major land reclamation programme.

▼ **Figure 2.50**
New agricultural land in Egypt.

The area of agricultural land was increased from 2.3 million hectares to 2.9 million hectares in the 1980s, and there are plans to reclaim a further 0.5 million hectares during the 1990s. It is hoped this will create 5 million extra jobs and homes for 800,000 families, and that as a result fewer people will want to leave the countryside.

Shortage of services: housing

Because of the speed of population growth, the provision of services has always run behind the needs of the population. Housing shortages are common, and there are few transport routes to the new areas on the edge of the city. There are not enough jobs for the working population. The following is one person's description of Cairo.

'Cairo: one could be excused for thinking that there are two cities bearing the same name. On the one hand the image is still alive of the Cairo of the 19th-century illustrators, a mysterious oriental bazaar where robed traders conducted their business in the shade of lofty medieval Islamic buildings. On the other hand there is the Cairo of the present day: a vast conurbation estimated to shelter some 12 to 14 million inhabitants, the largest city in Africa and the Middle East. This is a vision-come-true of rampant urbanism, perpetual traffic jams, overcrowding on a grand scale, with the homeless settling in what were once the cemeteries of the sultans, a sewage system under such pressure that it lifts the manholes, and apartment blocks that occasionally collapse under the weight of extra storeys.'

From the *Geographical Magazine*, September 1985

▼ **Figure 2.51**
Cairo.

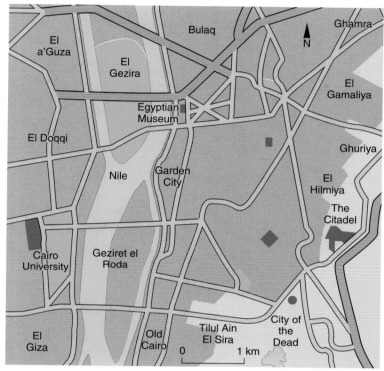

▼ **Figure 2.52**
In the City of the Dead.

Such pressures and shortages lead many people to what is called the **informal sector**. In terms of housing this means that people build their own homes using materials they are able to find. Such **spontaneous settlements** or shanty towns are found throughout the developing world. They often lack running water, electricity and mains drainage. In Cairo there are many areas, such as Bulaq and Chobra, which people have created for themselves. Others live in the 'City of the

Dead' – it has been estimated that as many as 3 million people may live in the tombs of this cemetery on the east of the city. New, isolated communities grow up on the edge of Cairo all the time. Wealthy people live close to the central area of the city – prosperous suburbs do not exist in the same way as in a developed country.

Egypt's answer

Several schemes have been devised to combat the housing problem. Tower blocks have been constructed to save space. However, they take time to build and many people cannot afford to rent them. Low-cost housing called 'site and service' schemes offer the land, a concrete base, and connections to water and sewerage systems. People then develop their own homes at their own pace. Nearly 1 million homes were built in this way between 1982 and 1986. Many of these were situated in 19 new towns. These are built in the desert where land is cheaper, and the hope is that they will attract people by providing reasonable homes and the prospect of employment (Figure 2.53). An average of 86 factories a year were opening in the new towns during this period.

▲ **Figure 2.53**
A new town in Egypt.

City	Planned population
10th of Ramadan City	500,000
Al Alam	250,000
El Ameriyya	1,000,000
6th October City	250,000
15th May City	150,000
Badry	250,000
Al Amal	250,000

Employment

Because of the jobs shortage, people often buy goods from wholesalers and then sell them from door to door or in the street markets. Others are involved in recycling the vast amounts of waste to be found in a city of this size. But it has been estimated that 60 per cent of the population are unemployed.

Egypt's answer

Egypt has developed its industries in order to create more jobs. It has used three strategies. Instead of selling goods like oil and cotton to other countries which then make things from them, Egypt is itself now manufacturing products from these resources. This adds value and creates jobs in factories. Secondly it has developed its tourist industry. The number of tourists doubled during the 1980s. This has meant new jobs in hotels and shops and at tourist attractions (Figure 2.54). Finally it has developed industries to create goods in order to cut down on imports such as building materials and vehicles. Altogether 350,000 jobs a year were created between 1981 and 1991.

▲ **Figure 2.54**
An Egyptian tourist attraction: Abu Simbel.

Activities

1 Analyse the case study on pages 55–59. Write a report which shows:

a the causes and

b the consequences

of rapid urban growth in Egypt. Your report must include a simple but useful sketch-map and a suitable graph to show the facts and figures.

2 a What is a primate city?

b How does a primate city come about?

c With the help of a good atlas, make two lists of primate cities – one for the North and one for the South.

3 a How has Egypt tried to reduce the dominance of Cairo?

b Find out how Nigeria and Brazil have tried to reduce the dominance of their primate cities.

4 Read the case study of Cairo, particularly the section on services. Remind yourself of the structure of cities in the developed world (see the models on page 35).

a Write two lists, one of the similarities and the other of the contrasts between cities in the developed world and the developing world.
(*Hint:* land use pattern, housing, services.)

b Describe two ways of providing housing for Cairo's poor. Which do you judge to be the better method? Why?

5 a From your knowledge of cities in the South, and referring particularly to the case study of Cairo in this unit, what do you consider will be the *likely* changes in cities in the developing world in the next 20 years?

b What changes would you *hope for* in the next 20 years? Why?

THINKING GEOGRAPHY

Looking for bias

As students of Geography we seek to *describe* and *explain* patterns that we find on the Earth. As we cannot visit everywhere ourselves we have to rely on the work of others. The way in which descriptions and explanations are presented has changed a great deal in the last 100 years. However the information is presented, we must remember that what we are shown has been *selected* by someone to reinforce the point they are making about a particular place or theory. In a way they come between us and what they are describing; they are said to be *mediating*. This is true of all the methods we use to convey an image of an area, e.g. photographs.

Writing

The person who wrote the following was keen to present a picture of power and spectacle:

'Nowhere is the magnificent and harmonious design of the planet more evident than at the meeting of raw red-hot magma and cold sea water.'

Volcano, Time Life Books, 1984

Someone who had lost their home in a volcanic eruption might not see it the same way.

Photographs

Authors of textbooks look for photos that show a good example of what they are trying to explain. This can lead to the use of stereotypes. We are presented with a 'typical' desert landscape (see above) or a 'typical' out-of-town shopping centre. It is important to think about just how typical they are. Not all deserts look like the ones in the photographs.

▲ *Different types of desert.*

Maps

As with writing and photos, maps are used to *describe* and *explain*. However, the information shown on the map has been selected. Why was this area chosen? What has been included and what has been left out? These are all important questions.

Statistics

One of the most familiar ways in which geographers prove a point is by using statistics. Thought needs to be given to *scale*. Will statistics at a national level in a large country tell us much about the lives of people in the different regions of that country? Do figures which tell us about average life expectancy or average earnings tell us much about the lives of the people in that country?

Satellite images

Surely there's no problem here? It's just picture taken by a machine out in space. If you look at the caption to a satellite image it may well say 'False colour image'. The colours have been chosen to make a particular point, for example to show the extent of river flooding, or the destruction of rainforests.

False colour satellite image in which colours have been used to show the destruction of the Brazilian rainforest to make way for human settlement.

Activities

The following questions ask you to detect, correct and then create bias yourself.

1 Look at Unit 2 of this book. Identify two or three maps or photographs where you think there is bias in the way information has been presented. Explain your selection.

2 For the information you have found, suggest a way that the information could be conveyed in another, fairer way.

3 Stereotypes are often used to help create a biased image. Using stereotypes, show how a place can be 'sold' as a holiday destination. Try to use real examples: a visit to the local travel agency and an examination of travel brochures may give you some ideas.

Geography and Ecology

This unit investigates questions and issues about the living world. The main ideas are summarised by the following focus statements:

- **Natural environments can be analysed as a collection of 'systems'.**

- **Ecosystems can be seen as a resource. If an ecosystem is destroyed, its resources of plant and animal life, and the soil, are lost – sometimes for ever.**

- **Ecosystems are dynamic and can undergo change.**

- **Some ecosystems are fragile and need special protection.**

- **Some ecosystems are managed by people. There is increasing interest in how to do this in a sustainable way.**

To examine these ideas we include examples from Africa (Lake Victoria, Zimbabwe, Mali and Burkina Faso), China, Brazil, the USA and Britain.

Systems and ecosystems

Systems

People use the word 'systems' in many different ways. For example, we talk of the **school system** or a **hi-fi system**. Large cities have **transport systems**. The Post Office has a **distribution system**.

A system can be defined as: *anything formed of parts placed together in a connected whole.* Therefore a hi-fi system is made up of several parts, or components. Together the amplifier, speakers and CD player make up a system that allows us to listen to music.

A system can be divided into four parts: inputs, flows, stores and outputs. Think about the energy that goes into making a hi-fi system work. The electricity enters the system when you switch on, and most flows through the system to make it work. Energy was also used to make the various components and plastic: this is stored in the system. The energy output is transformed into what we recognise as music.

▼ **Figure 3.1**
A hi-fi system.

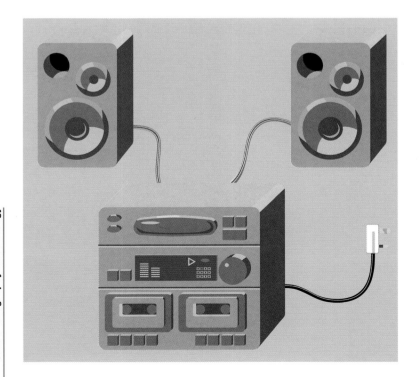

We can divide systems into artificial and natural systems. The hi-fi is an example of an artificial system, whilst a tree is an example of a natural system.

Activities

1 Make a copy of the following table, and add as many examples as you can to your copy.

System	Natural or artificial
Hi-fi	Artificial
A tree	Natural

2 Choose one of the systems from your table, and draw a systems diagram. Show the inputs, flows, stores and outputs as different colours. **Figure 3.2** will help you to get started.

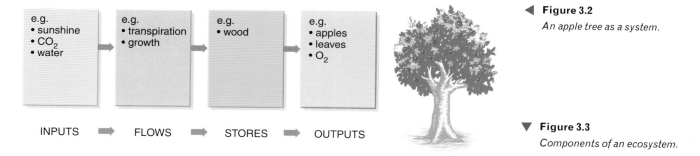

e.g.	e.g.	e.g.	e.g.
• sunshine	• transpiration	• wood	• apples
• CO_2	• growth		• leaves
• water			• O_2

INPUTS ⟹ FLOWS ⟹ STORES ⟹ OUTPUTS

◀ **Figure 3.2**
An apple tree as a system.

▼ **Figure 3.3**
Components of an ecosystem.

Ecosystems

Ecosystems are examples of environmental systems. *Eco* is the Greek word for 'home'. Figure 3.3 shows the components and links in an ecosystem. As you can see, the system can be divided into the living and non-living environment. Ecosystems work on a variety of scales: they can be as small as a hedgerow or pond, or as large as a tropical rainforest. This larger type of ecosystem is known as a **biome**. The planet Earth as a whole can be seen as a global ecosystem. All the living components of the global ecosystem – plants, animals, people and microbes – are called the **biosphere**.

To show how productive a part of the global ecosystem is, the term **biomass** is used. This is the weight of all living things produced in a given area.

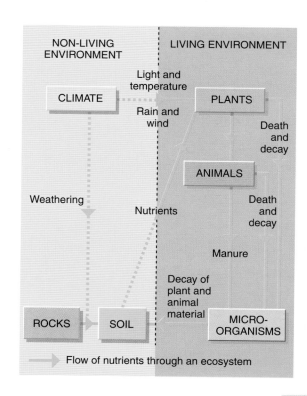

NON-LIVING ENVIRONMENT   LIVING ENVIRONMENT

CLIMATE

Light and temperature

PLANTS

Rain and wind

Death and decay

ANIMALS

Weathering

Nutrients

Death and decay

Manure

Decay of plant and animal material

ROCKS   SOIL

MICRO-ORGANISMS

⟶ Flow of nutrients through an ecosystem

The components of an ecosystem are linked by **flows** of materials and energy. Water and carbon are two such types of material. They are *inputs* to the system, and can flow through the ecosystem. Sometimes they are stored for a while, and often they are changed by processes at work in the ecosystem. Eventually they move on around the system – this is called **feedback**. Sometimes they leave the system altogether as **outputs**.

Water passing through the ecosystem has two important jobs: it provides the moisture needed by living plants and animals, and it carries nutrients (food) wanted by them. The energy that drives water and nutrients through the system comes from the sun. Figure 3.4 shows two cycles: the water cycle and the carbon cycle. Carbon is a vital element in all living systems, providing the basic building block for the growth of living things. When vegetation dies, the carbon is often stored for a long time: today's coal and oilfields represent carbon that was stored in living things millions of years ago.

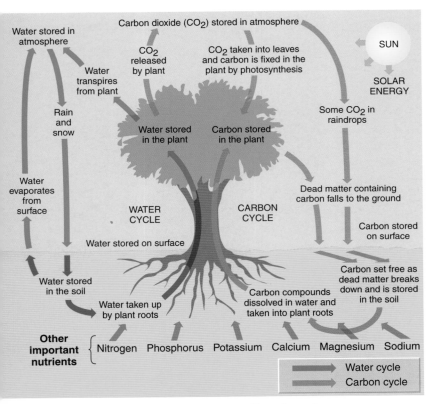

Figure 3.4

Water and carbon cycles through an ecosystem.

Activities

Make a copy of **Figure 3.4**.

1 Describe two ways in which trees and other plants take up carbon.

2 Name two stores of carbon in the ecosystem.

3 Give an example of a 'feedback' from the carbon cycle.

4 Describe the parts of the carbon cycle in which water is very important.

5 'Water does not just carry carbon, but also other nutrients such as nitrogen and phosphorus.' Explain what could happen to these nutrient cycles if there was a drought.

Food webs

In an ecosystem, energy in the form of food can pass from one living creature to another. The sun's energy is used by green plants to produce plant material from air, water and minerals in the soil (this process is known as **photosynthesis**). Green plants are therefore called **producers**. These plants can be consumed by plant-eating animals, or herbivores (**consumers**). Other animals may eat the herbivores. These consumers are called carnivores. Some animals eat plants *and* animals, and are called omnivores. This pattern of consumption is called a **food chain**. In any ecosystem there are many food chains resulting in a more complicated **food web**.

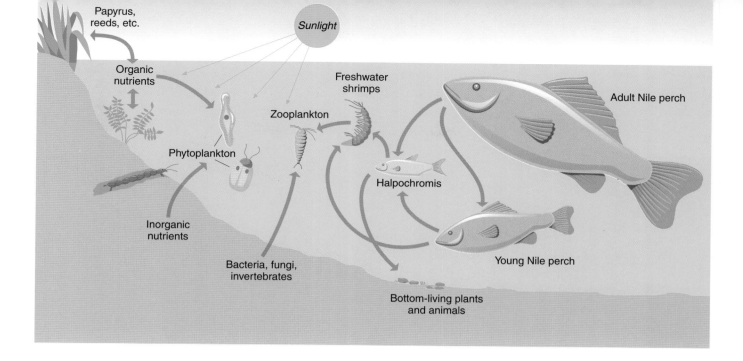

Labels within figure:
Papyrus, reeds, etc.
Sunlight
Organic nutrients
Freshwater shrimps
Adult Nile perch
Zooplankton
Phytoplankton
Halpochromis
Inorganic nutrients
Young Nile perch
Bacteria, fungi, invertebrates
Bottom-living plants and animals

Figure 3.5 shows a food web for the animals and plants living in Lake Victoria, in East Africa. It shows how the creatures in the lake are interdependent, as there are many chains linking them.

There is a succession of feeding. Producers, such as the reeds, papyrus and other plants, are eaten by primary consumers such as the zooplankton. These are eaten by fish called Halpochromis, which are secondary consumers. At the top of the food web is a fish called the Nile perch, a predator and a tertiary consumer.

The Nile perch was introduced into Lake Victoria by people in the 1960s, with the intention of creating a fishing industry and a source of fish protein for local people to eat. The perch spread quite quickly, and because individual fish grew as large as 2 m in length, weighing up to 200 kg, the experiment seemed to be successful. However, the fish had a huge impact on the lake ecosystem, because it affected the numbers of Halpochromis, which in turn affected the numbers of other living organisms in the lake. Some idea of the extent of this impact is shown by figures for the food chain: in order to gain 1 kg in weight, the Nile perch has to eat 4 kg of Halpochromis, and Halpochromis itself needs to eat 40 kg of zooplankton to put on weight. Thus, for a time, the introduction of the Nile perch threw the lake ecosystem out of balance. It is now beginning adjust to its new state. The people who introduced the Nile perch never imagined they would change the lake ecosystem for ever. Introduction of the perch almost destroyed the food chain and caused the collapse of local animal populations.

▲ **Figure 3.5**
Food web for Lake Victoria, in East Africa.

Activities

1 Draw your own food chain of Lake Victoria to show the direction of the flow of energy as it passes from producers through to tertiary consumers. You should present your diagram as a flow diagram, using arrows to present energy flows, and boxes for the examples of the types of consumer.

2 You have been asked by a nature conservation group to help people living in the region of Lake Victoria to understand the impact of the Nile perch. Design a diagram or poster. It should include information about the food chain, and explain why the animal populations in the lake almost collapsed.

Comparing three ecosystems

Appearance	Climate	Biomass

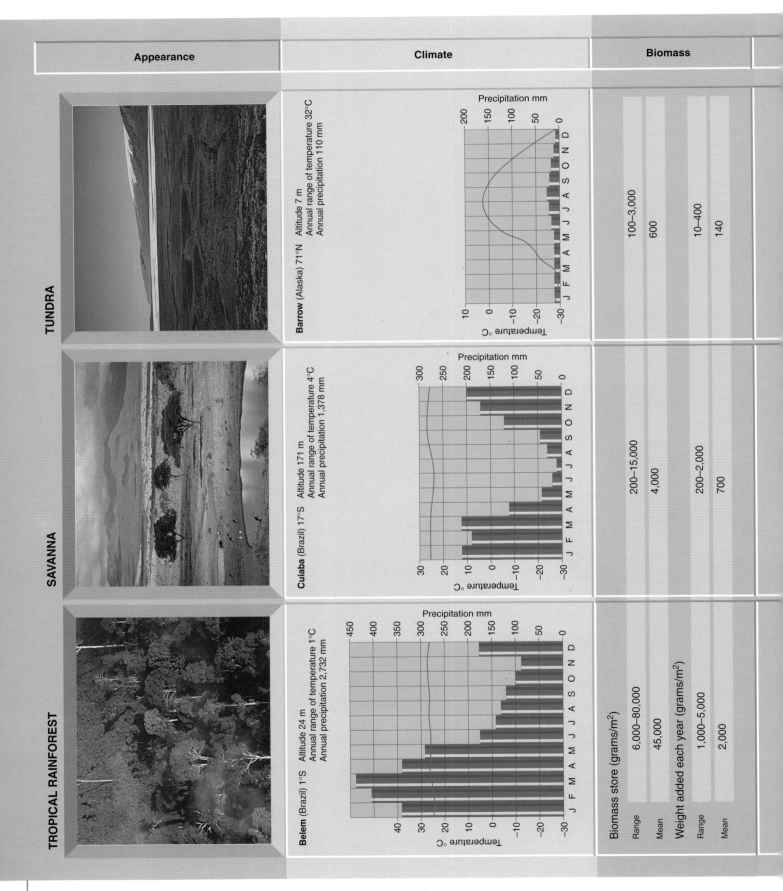

TUNDRA

Barrow (Alaska) 71°N   Altitude 7 m
Annual range of temperature 32°C
Annual precipitation 110 mm

Precipitation mm

Temperature °C

SAVANNA

Cuiaba (Brazil) 17°S   Altitude 171 m
Annual range of temperature 4°C
Annual precipitation 1,378 mm

Precipitation mm

Temperature °C

TROPICAL RAINFOREST

Belem (Brazil) 1°S   Altitude 24 m
Annual range of temperature 1°C
Annual precipitation 2,732 mm

Precipitation mm

Temperature °C

Biomass store (grams/m²)

	Range	Mean
Tundra	100–3,000	600
Savanna	200–15,000	4,000
Tropical rainforest	6,000–80,000	45,000

Weight added each year (grams/m²)

	Range	Mean
Tundra	10–400	140
Savanna	200–2,000	700
Tropical rainforest	1,000–5,000	2,000

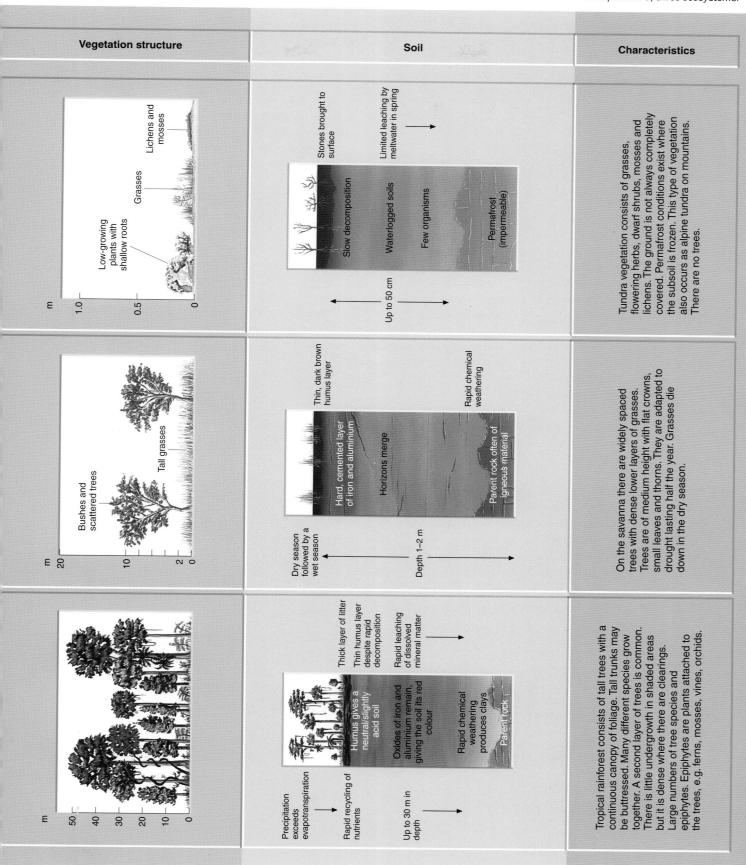

Vegetation structure	Soil	Characteristics

Tundra

Vegetation structure: m — 1.0, 0.5, 0 — Low-growing plants with shallow roots; Grasses; Lichens and mosses

Soil: Up to 50 cm — Stones brought to surface; Limited leaching by meltwater in spring; Slow decomposition; Waterlogged soils; Few organisms; Permafrost (impermeable)

Characteristics: Tundra vegetation consists of grasses, flowering herbs, dwarf shrubs, mosses and lichens. The ground is not always completely covered. Permafrost conditions exist where the subsoil is frozen. This type of vegetation also occurs as alpine tundra on mountains. There are no trees.

Savanna

Vegetation structure: m — 20, 10, 2, 0 — Bushes and scattered trees; Tall grasses

Soil: Dry season followed by a wet season; Depth 1–2 m — Thin, dark brown humus layer; Hard, cemented layer of iron and aluminium; Horizons merge; Rapid chemical weathering; Parent rock often of igneous material

Characteristics: On the savanna there are widely spaced trees with dense lower layers of grasses. Trees are of medium height with flat crowns, small leaves and thorns. They are adapted to drought lasting half the year. Grasses die down in the dry season.

Tropical rainforest

Vegetation structure: m — 50, 40, 30, 20, 10, 0

Soil: Precipitation exceeds evapotranspiration; Rapid recycling of nutrients; Up to 30 m in depth — Thick layer of litter; Thin humus layer despite rapid decomposition; Rapid leaching of dissolved mineral matter; Humus gives a neutral/slightly acid soil; Oxides of iron and aluminium remain, giving the soil its red colour; Rapid chemical weathering produces clays; Parent rock

Characteristics: Tropical rainforest consists of tall trees with a continuous canopy of foliage. Tall trunks may be buttressed. Many different species grow together. A second layer of trees is common. There is little undergrowth in shaded areas but it is dense where there are clearings. Large numbers of tree species and epiphytes. Epiphytes are plants attached to the trees, e.g. ferns, mosses, vines, orchids.

Quite suddenly you find yourself inside a majestic cathedral, the height of a seventeen-storey building. You are immediately dwarfed by the sheer immensity of the biomass. Your senses are ambushed by the thick scent of decay. The smells are exciting and make you feel a bit drunk.

Your eyes take a few moments to adjust to this world which is forever twilight. Almost everything is a sombre shade of green apart from the odd brilliant electric-blue flash of a huge Morpho butterfly. It is hot and humid – do anything remotely energetic and you feel exhausted.

The forest floor

Down here on the forest floor no breeze can be felt. The trees above are such good protection that you do not really know that it is raining on the trees above you until five minutes after the storm has started. There are times of the year when every afternoon there is a torrential downpour of rain, making leaves drip and glisten with water. Little sunlight reaches through to the forest floor. Because of this there is very little undergrowth deep in the forest. The only use for a machete here is not to hack your way through, but to leave your trail marked. It is easy to get disoriented and lost in a rainforest.

The shrub layer

The interior of the forest is a magical place. In the canopy, scarlet macaws and spider monkeys disturb the leaves and branches. Lower down you can find Hercules beetles, armadillos and poison-arrow frogs. A single hectare of rainforest may contain 42,000 different species of insect, 750 types of tree, and 1,500 species of other plants. With such richness the rainforest is one of the planet's most astounding expressions of life.

The canopy

The tallest trees (emergents) tower to a height of 60 or 84 metres, piercing the main canopy which is about 37 metres high. The bases of the larger and medium-sized trees send out massive buttresses or supports which help keep the trees secure in strong winds. The tree canopy is laced with vines or lianas, some of which can be as much as 244 metres long.

Adapted from A. Newman, Tropical Rainforest, 1990

Figure 3.7 *The world's living cathedral: the tropical rainforest.*

Activities

1 Using **Figure 3.6** on pages 66–67, study the systems for savanna and tundra ecosystems. Look at the photographs for all three ecosystems. Then also using the information in **Figure 3.7**, design and draw your own diagram of a rainforest ecosystem. Your diagram needs to show the structure of the forest layers.

2 a Explain what the word *biomass* means.

 b What is the difference between range of biomass stored and weight gained, and the mean for each of these?

 c Which of the three ecosystems is most productive? Explain your answer.

3 Work with a partner, and study the typical soil profiles for each of the three systems. Decide which is the most fertile soil, and rank each soil in order of fertility. Justify (explain) your ranking.

Extension activities

4 a What is the relationship between the types of soil and the vegetation? Explain your answer.

 b Huge amounts of energy and nutrients are contained within the tropical rainforest ecosystem. But where is most of this energy stored: in the soil, or in the vegetation? Justify your answer.

5 Make a list of all the things that you think might make some ecosystems more fragile than others (that is, more easily harmed). Using your list, decide which of the three ecosystems – rainforest, savanna or tundra – is the most fragile. Give reasons for your choice.

Ecosystems on the world map: the biomes

We can imagine the world being made up of different, large-scale ecosystems, some water-based, some land-based, a bit like a jigsaw puzzle. But why are there different types of ecosystem? By looking at the distribution of biomes and comparing these with climate patterns, we can begin to investigate the links between climate at a global scale and the development of biomes. The climate determines the inputs to the ecosystem.

▼ **Figure 3.8**
Some of the world's major areas of natural vegetation.

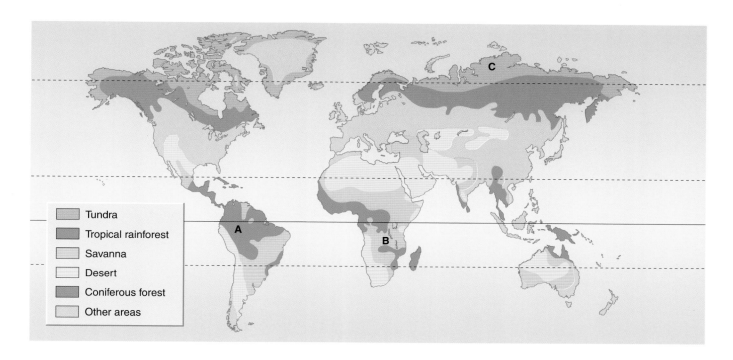

Tundra
Tropical rainforest
Savanna
Desert
Coniferous forest
Other areas

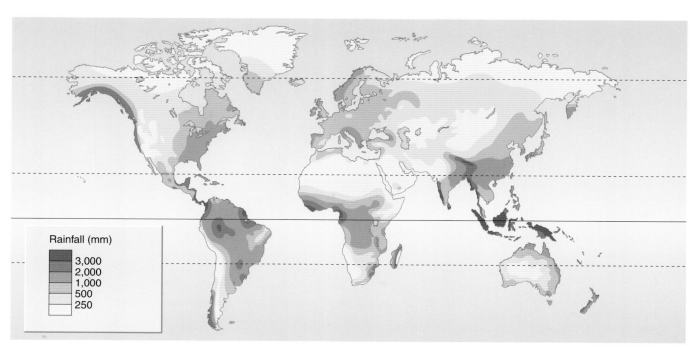

Rainfall (mm)
3,000
2,000
1,000
500
250

▲ **Figure 3.9** *World annual precipitation.*

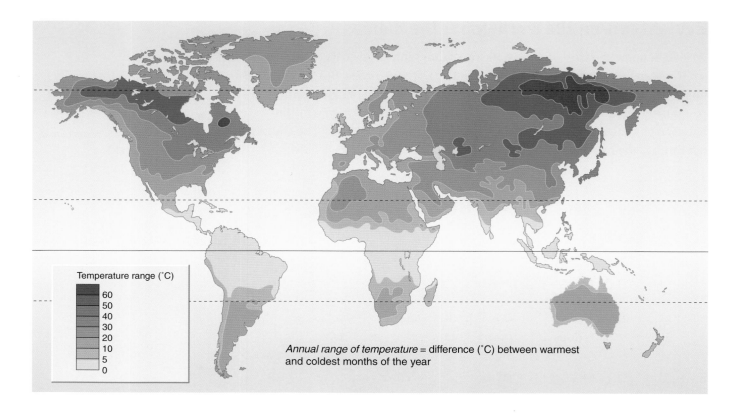

Temperature range (°C)

60
50
40
30
20
10
5
0

Annual range of temperature = difference (°C) between warmest and coldest months of the year

▲ **Figure 3.10**

Annual global range of temperature.

Activities

1 For each of the biomes in the list below, describe its world distribution. Use these headings to guide you: *Latitude, Continents, Examples of countries in which the biome is present.*

- Rainforest
- Savanna
- Tundra
- Desert
- Coniferous forest

2 a Using **Figures 3.8–3.10** to help you, copy and complete the following table for the three biomes described in **Figure 3.6**.

Location (see Figure 3.8)	Temperature (annual range)	Precipitation (annual average)	Vegetation type
A			
B			
C			

b Identify the links between the type of vegetation, precipitation and temperature. Explain why the links you identify are important.

Ecosystems and resources

Throughout history people have made use of **natural resources** to meet their needs. People are motivated to identify and find resources for three main reasons:

- The need for food.

- The need to make things for everyday use, such as materials to build with.

- The need to enjoy themselves.

Many of the living and non-living components of the Earth have been used by people.

People's use of resources has increased greatly during the 19th and 20th centuries, causing damage to ecosystems. Groups such as Greenpeace and Friends of the Earth have succeeded in bringing ecological issues to the front pages of our newspapers. They have highlighted the need to make sure that our use of resources does not lead to damaging changes to ecosystems. They have helped introduce new ideas to people, such as 'sustainable development', 'conservation', and 'stewardship' (Figure 3.11).

This topic could become a GCSE geographical enquiry. If you choose to do this, your two-minute script prepared for the Extension activity (see below) could become the Conclusion of your enquiry report.

▼ **Figure 3.11**

Caring for our ecosystems.

Activities

1 Make a copy of the chart below, and fill in the columns. You will find relevant information by quickly reading through other units in this book. A good atlas will also help you.

Natural resources and human needs					
Sphere example	Components	Uses	Human needs met	Conflicts	Named example
Atmosphere	Upper				
	Lower				
Biosphere	Grassland				
	Agricultural land				
	Wilderness				
	Forests				
Hydrosphere	Fresh water				

Extension activity

2 Prepare a script for a two-minute TV report about damage to a local ecosystem caused by exploitation of resources. Use an issue you have seen reported, or research an ecosystem close to where you live. It may be possible for you to use a video camera to record your report.

• **Sustainable development**
Progress or development which meets our needs without leaving future generations with fewer resources and more environmental problems – that is, development can be sustained for ever.

• **Conservation**
Managing resources so that they remain intact for future generations. Conservation usually means that ecosystems must be managed in some way: for example, it is illegal to catch more than a certain limited quota of fish from the North Sea.

• **Stewardship**
The idea that we have the responsibility of holding the environment 'in trust' for future generations. Stewardship requires that every development – building houses, factories and roads, or how offices and schools are organised and run – is 'tested' for its sustainability.

Natural changes in ecosystems

We have seen that the world map is made up of a jigsaw of different ecosystems, and that climate is the main influence on the distribution of biomes. At a local scale, the influence of climate is less clear-cut. By looking at a small sand-dune ecosystem, we can investigate what factors give the ecosystem its character, and how these factors change in space (from place to place), and over time.

Craig Weightman is a geography teacher. Each year he runs a field course for students to North Devon. One of the investigations that he and his students carry out is on a sand-dune ecosystem. In Figure 3.12 he tells us a little bit more about this enquiry.

The point in Craig's last sentence about how sand dunes change naturally with distance from the sea is an important one. The page from Craig's notebook shown in Figure 3.13 makes this idea of change with distance a bit clearer.

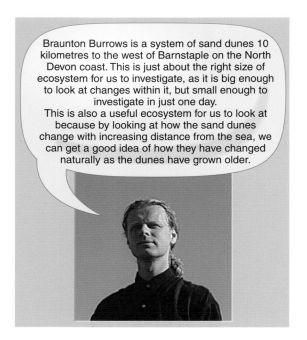

> Braunton Burrows is a system of sand dunes 10 kilometres to the west of Barnstaple on the North Devon coast. This is just about the right size of ecosystem for us to investigate, as it is big enough to look at changes within it, but small enough to investigate in just one day.
> This is also a useful ecosystem for us to look at because by looking at how the sand dunes change with increasing distance from the sea, we can get a good idea of how they have changed naturally as the dunes have grown older.

▲ **Figure 3.12**

Introducing Craig Weightman.

▼ **Figure 3.13**

Pages from Craig's field notebook.

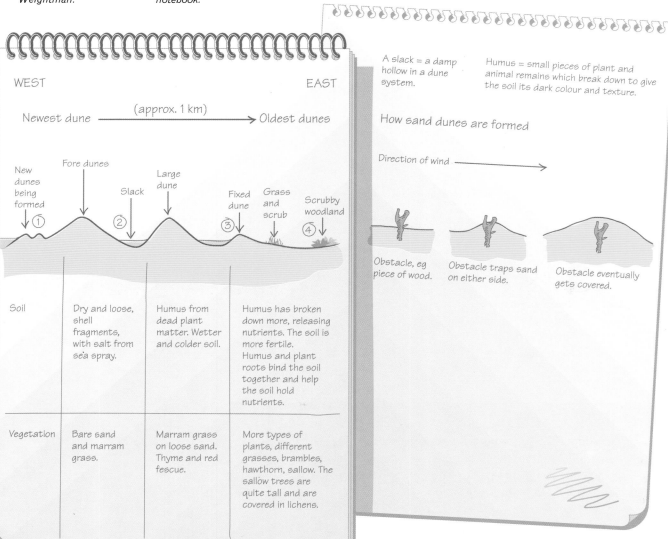

Activities

Refer to **Figure 3.13**.

1 a From which direction is the prevailing wind at Braunton Burrows?

b Describe the location of the newest and oldest sand dunes.

c With reference to Craig's notebook, explain why the newest and oldest dunes are where they are.

2 On his last visit to Braunton Burrows, Craig took the photographs shown in **Figure 3.14**. Match each of the photographs labelled A to D with the four points marked 1 to 4 on Craig's cross-section of the dune system (**Figure 3.13**).

3 Using all the information in **Figures 3.13** and **3.14**, describe how the following things change as you move inland across the dunes:

- the amount of soil/sand left bare
- the numbers and different types of plants
- the height of the vegetation
- the number of layers of different height in the vegetation
- the soil characteristics.

▼ **Figure 3.14**
Different parts of the sand-dune ecosystem.

The process we have observed in this sand-dune ecosystem is called **plant succession**. This is a natural process. Left to themselves, the dunes of Braunton Burrows change. Once the new dunes are created, it is a matter of time before marram grass begins to grow on them. The marram grass changes the dune a little, for example adding humus to the soil. This small change allows other plants like thyme and other grasses to move in (to **succeed**). These new plants change the dune a little more, so that new plants and animals can move in, and allowing further succession.

Figure 3.15
People and sand dunes: measures taken to control erosion.

Damage caused by people at Braunton Burrows is a real concern because the area is a designated nature reserve. A particular worry is the damage caused by people's feet, as they can quickly wear away marram grass, leaving the sand free to be blown away by the wind.

Activities

1 a What could happen to the sand dunes if they were not protected?

b What can be done to help protect these fragile ecosystems?

2 Each year Craig produces a booklet for his Year 10 students, on the sand dunes at Braunton Burrows. Write a paragraph for this booklet – not more than a single side of A4 paper – explaining why it is important to understand what the ecosystem is like, and the natural changes taking place there. You will need to explain that the dunes need to be looked after or managed. Try to present the information attractively so that students are encouraged to read it.

Soil erosion: a worldwide problem

Soil is vital to ecosystems. All over the world, soil is increasingly under threat from human interference such as forestry or farming. In some more fragile ecosystems, particularly at desert fringes, soil needs to be protected if it is to remain intact for use by future generations. This section investigates where and why accelerated **soil erosion** is happening, and explores some of the solutions.

Soil is a source of the plant foods (nutrients) on which farming depends. Accelerated erosion happens when more soil is removed by either wind or water than is made by natural processes such as the weathering of rock. Each year 75 million tonnes of topsoil are lost in the world.

Soil erosion in Britain has increased over the past 20 years. One-third of arable land in England and Wales (25,000 km²) is at risk from erosion. Soil is eroded when rainwater on slopes collects in small channels or **rills**. As the water runs off it gathers speed, carrying soil particles. Erosion is a particular problem when fields are bare or have little vegetation cover after they have been ploughed.

The speed of soil erosion is affected by the type of soil and the local farming practices. For example, the thin, chalky soils found in southern and south-east England are vulnerable, and it is in this area that farming has been intensified, with farmers trying to increase the yields from their land to make a bigger profit. One way they have achieved this is by ploughing the land in late summer and sowing crops in the autumn rather than in the spring. This practice leaves fields bare or with little vegetation cover at a time when rainfall is heavy and **run-off** likely to be at a high level. The use of more powerful machinery also compacts the soil, encouraging run-off in the tyre tracks. Ploughs now dig much deeper, breaking up the soil into finer pieces, which are more easily eroded. Improvements to farm equipment mean that steeper slopes can be cultivated, where run-off can be faster and more damaging. Larger fields without hedges or banks to slow down run-off mean that rills can develop into much larger **gullies**.

Under the conditions of the British climate, accelerated erosion is unlikely to happen where there is good vegetation cover. However, it is becoming a problem because of current farming practices, and in certain areas these need to change. Farmers need to be made more aware of the problem, and encouraged to deal with it.

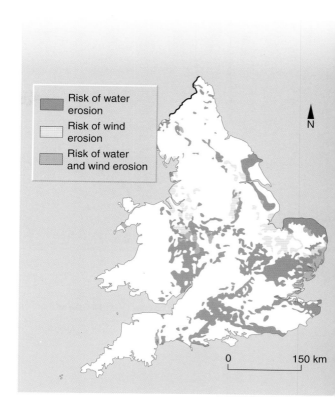

	Risk of water erosion
	Risk of wind erosion
	Risk of water and wind erosion

▲ **Figure 3.16**
Land most at risk from soil erosion in England and Wales.

▼ **Figure 3.17**
Gully created during a storm, in a field in Fife, Scotland.

Unit 3 **Geography and Ecology**

Activities

1 In what ways is soil a vital part of the ecosystem?

2 What is soil erosion?

3 What factors make soil erosion more of a problem in some areas of the world than others? Use real examples to illustrate your answer.

▲ **Figure 3.18**
Soil erosion on a large scale, in the Dustbowl of the USA in the 1930s.

Figure 3.19
Case study: The collapse of farming in the mid-west USA.

During the 1930s the American mid-west became a dustbowl (see Figure 3.18). Over-cultivation, drought and strong winds caused thousands of tonnes of topsoil to be whipped off, and thousands of people had to leave their homes and their land. Today, in the 1990s, these states of North and South Dakota, Nebraska and parts of Wyoming are in crisis once again.

Meteorologists from the Department of Agriculture report that rainfall is too low to support agriculture. The minimum rainfall needed for farming in the region is 20 inches. The average rainfall in recent years has been between 13.11 and 19.2 inches. To survive, farmers have been irrigating their crops with water taken from the vast underground Ogallala Aquifer. However, supplies are dwindling, and the US Geological Survey predicts that by the year 2000 water from the aquifer will have sunk so low that it will be too expensive and too difficult to extract. Without water little grows, and the soil becomes exposed to erosion by wind and water.

The resulting collapse in agriculture has its human cost. The Farmers' Home Administration in South Dakota reports that 50 farmers abandoned their farms completely last year. In Nebraska, there are now fewer than 4 people per square mile, and more than 20% of people live in poverty. For many it takes a journey of 50 miles to reach the nearest doctor or shop.

To continue to farm where there is not enough rain could be a human as well as an ecological disaster ...

From the *Geographical Magazine*, October 1990

Figure 3.20
Case study: Over-grazing in Africa.

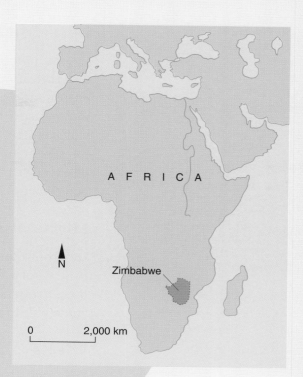

About 80,000 hectares of Zimbabwean land was deforested annually during the 1980s. This trend is expected to continue. In Nigeria that figure is 400,000 hectares, and in Zaire 347,000 hectares. The loss of those trees means that many types of forest vegetation and wildlife will vanish. Without the web created by the trees' root system, Africa's soil erosion problem is expected to become a serious crisis.

The over-grazing of land by domesticated cattle and goats also causes soil erosion. In parts of Zimbabwe, the size of the cattle herd reflects a family's wealth and status. As a result, there are often more cattle in a herd than the land can safely support. This 'cash on the hoof' is usually owned by the wealthy, who pay poorer villagers to herd them. In addition, the growing of inappropriate crops, such as moisture-loving maize in semi-arid areas, and poor tilling methods, further degrade the land.

- Desertification affects one-sixth of the world's population.
- 3.6 billion hectares of the world's land surface area is affected by desertification.
- Every year an area of land the size of Britain is either lost or severely degraded.
- In Africa alone, 61 million people are affected by desertification.

Desertification

In some parts of the world, soil erosion is just one part of a larger story of **desertification** and land degradation. Desertification can happen in very dry environments; although the land was once productive, it becomes unproductive and desert-like. The processes involved include soil erosion which is often the result of over-grazing, over-cultivation, and the cutting of trees for fuelwood. The problem is particularly acute in the arid **Sahel** (or desert edge) areas of Africa, where economic pressures, population increase and climatic change all contribute to the overloading of a fragile ecosystem.

Effects on people

Desertification is slow and insidious. Developing countries suffer the most. Here, rural communities become trapped in a cycle of poverty which forces them to exploit the land beyond its **carrying capacity** – this makes it very vulnerable to drought and soil erosion.

Effects on climate

Desertification increases the amount of dust in the atmosphere. Scientists believe that as a result, air is prevented from rising freely to form convection clouds. The loss of vegetation reduces the amount of moisture in the air, causing surface temperatures to rise. Both of these factors make drought worse.

▶ Figure 3.22

Rainfall at Timbuktu, Mali, in the Sahel.

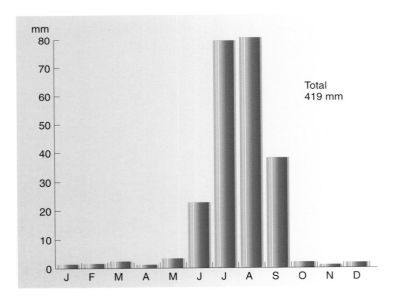

Activities

1 Produce a page for Year 8 students explaining in writing what desertification is and how it is caused. You will need to keep your audience in mind, and make sure your explanation is well planned, clear and interesting.

2 To what extent is desertification a problem caused by people, by natural processes, or by both? Use factual evidence to support your argument.

Figure 3.23

Case study: Green shoots in the sand – Burkina Faso.

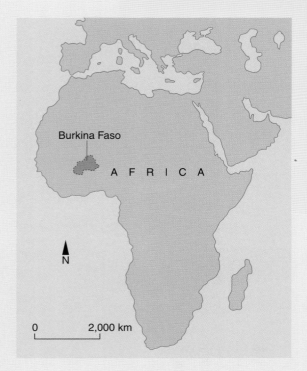

Throughout Burkina Faso, in villages such as Issigi and Korrabagre, local people are trying to halt the process of desertification. They plant trees, build dams and wells, create market gardens, build warehouses and set up 'cereal banks'. They make netting to combat soil erosion, and watering-cans for their gardens. Bernard Ouedraogo, who set up the project, says it is successful because 'it involves local people using traditional village organisations to help themselves. It is not a project thought up in the developed world and then imposed on the people.'

From *The Independent on Sunday*, 10 January 1993

Figure 3.24

Case study: Checkmate stalls desert advance in China.

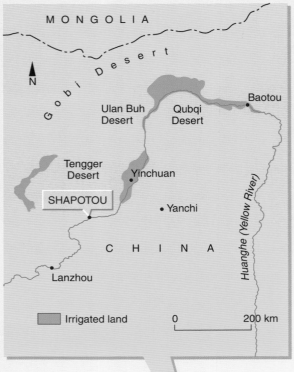

At the Shapotou Research Station in the Tengger Desert, the first stage in desert reclamation has been to set up a windbreak made of willow or bamboo. Behind this barrier straw 'checkerboards' are constructed. These increase surface roughness, slowing down the wind and stabilising the sand. These checkerboards stay in place for up to five years, enough time for plants that are able to withstand very dry conditions to get established.

These plants add moisture to the air through transpiration, and organic matter to the soil, encouraging more vegetation.

From the *Geographical Magazine*, November 1991

Activity

The charity Green Deserts has asked you to produce some educational materials for their fieldworkers in desertified areas in India and Africa. The materials are to be used to educate farmers about desertification. You will need to keep in mind that few of the farmers speak English, and most are not literate. Your materials must cover three areas:

- What desertification is and how it is caused.

- Its short-term and long-term environmental and human effects.

- Advice on possible solutions.

Use all the information in this section to help you prepare your materials.

Managing an ecosystem: Rondonia in the Amazon rainforest

This section helps us to apply what we have learned about ecosystems. In all parts of the world people must make decisions about how to manage ecosystems. Here we investigate what is happening to the rainforest in Rondonia, a state of Brazil (Figure 3.25). Especially important is the role of new farmers and their impact on the ecosystem. You will be in role to advise these new farmers and the government on what could be done to make a living from the rainforest without damaging or even destroying large areas of it for ever. First though you need to know a bit about what is happening in Rondonia.

The state of Rondonia has some of the fastest rates of deforestation in Brazil. These appear to be linked to an equally fast growth in the area's population (Figure 3.26). Despite controls introduced by the Brazilian government in the late 1980s, recent evidence has shown that deforestation began to increase again in 1991. In 1996 the government introduced a two-year ban on the cutting of the two most important hardwoods, mahogany and virola. The amount of private land that can be deforested was also reduced from a half to a fifth.

Much of this increase in population and deforestation was because the government encouraged poor and landless people from other parts of Brazil to move into the rainforest. This migration, along with other changes, has put the rainforest ecosystem under threat. The trees were cut down and, without their store of nutrients and the protection of their branches and roots, the soils quickly became impoverished.

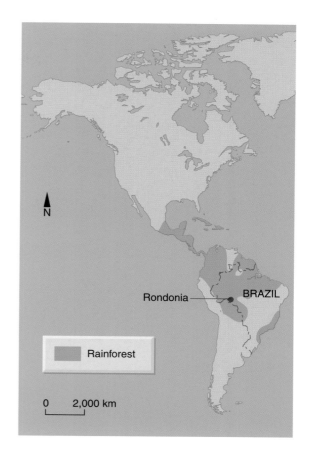

▲ **Figure 3.25**
The Brazilian rainforest.

▼ **Figure 3.26**
Deforestation and population growth in the state of Rondonia, 1970– 88.

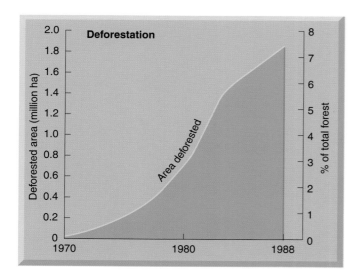

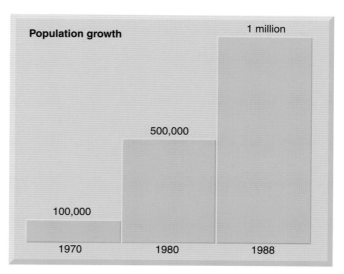

Figure 3.27

Change in Rondonia.

A *International timber logging.*

B *Cattle ranching.*

C *Mining activities.*

D *New settlements.*

E *New roads.*

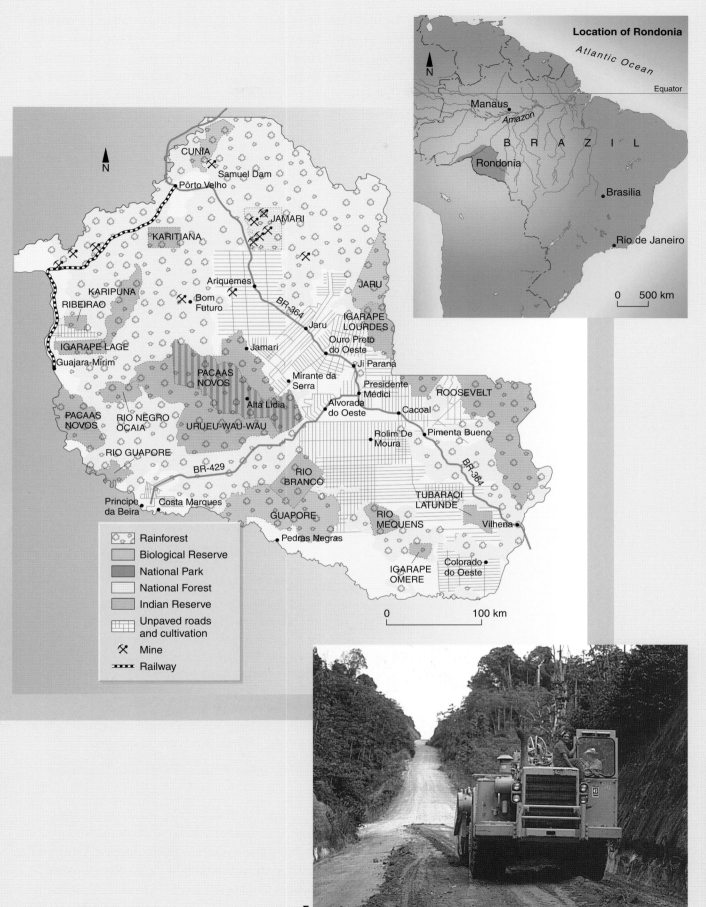

Location of Rondonia

Atlantic Ocean

Equator

Manaus
Amazon
B R A Z I L
Rondonia
Brasilia
Rio de Janeiro

0   500 km

N

CUNIA
Samuel Dam
Pôrto Velho
JAMARI
KARITIANA
KARIPUNA
RIBEIRAO
Ariquemes
Bom Futuro
BR-364
Jaru
JARU
IGARAPE LOURDES
Ouro Preto do Oeste
Jamari
Ji Paraná
IGARAPE LAGE
Guajara-Mirim
PACAAS NOVOS
Mirante da Serra
Presidente Médici
ROOSEVELT
Alta Lidia
Alvorada do Oeste
Cacoal
PACAAS NOVOS
RIO NEGRO OCAIA
URUEU-WAU-WAU
Rolim De Moura
Pimenta Bueno
RIO GUAPORE
BR-429
BR-364
RIO BRANCO
TUBARAOI LATUNDE
Principe da Beira
Costa Marques
GUAPORE
RIO MEQUENS
Vilhena
Pedras Negras
IGARAPE OMERE
Colorado do Oeste

Legend:
- Rainforest
- Biological Reserve
- National Park
- National Forest
- Indian Reserve
- Unpaved roads and cultivation
- ✕ Mine
- Railway

0   100 km

E

This threat to the rainforest ecosystem is important for a number of reasons. On a global scale its destruction would reduce biodiversity. Many species of plants and animals could be lost for ever. Without the rainforest, patterns of weather and climate could change. In some places up to 40 per cent less rain could fall, and daily temperatures could become much higher. See Figure 3.27.

▶ **Figure 3.27**
The world's rainforests and the water cycle.

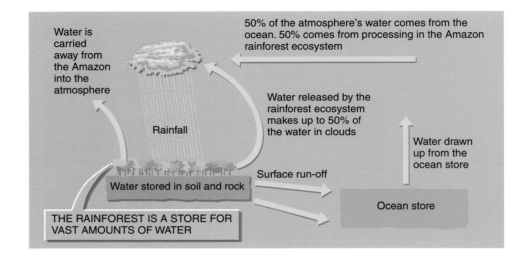

▶ **Figure 3.28**
Jose's story.

Jose is typical of the poor farmers who came to Rondonia to try to make a living from farming an area of land. His story is told by a Brazilian forest ecologist.

'The main crop he grows is manioc. It meets some of the food needs of his family, but not all of them. He first cleared a patch of land about three years ago but the soil soon became infertile and he had to move on. He is now clearing a new area by the "slash and burn" method. He chops down and burns the trees. The ash from the burning fertilises the soil for a while but without the protection of the trees and vegetation the rain soon washes the ash and the topsoil away. What we have to understand is that nearly all the nutrients in a tropical forest ecosystem are in the trees themselves. If you destroy the trees, you impoverish the ecosystem.'

Many scientists from all over the world have studied the Amazon rainforest. Katherine da Silva has been carrying out research into the effects of deforestation in Rondonia. The impact of incoming farmers is her special interest. She drew the picture in Figure 3.29 (page 85) when she was in Rondonia. It shows the kind of damage caused by farming practices that are not sensitive to the environment. Katherine has labelled her drawing to give an idea of the impact of deforestation.

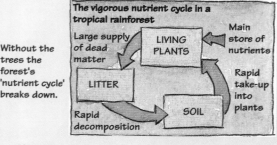

Thinner, less fertile soil means that crops cannot be grown for long before the patch has to be abandoned and a new area of rainforest cleared.

Landslides and 'slumps' may be caused on slopes which are no longer protected by trees.

The more fertile topsoil is the first to be washed away.

Soil washed into rivers can 'choke' them. Raised riverbed levels can cause flooding in areas far away from the area actually being deforested.

There are fewer trees to take up water, so increasing surface run-off.

Without the trees the forest's 'nutrient cycle' breaks down.

The vigorous nutrient cycle in a tropical rainforest

Large supply of dead matter → LIVING PLANTS ← Main store of nutrients

LITTER → SOIL

Rapid take-up into plants

Rapid decomposition

No trees are left to intercept the rain.

No trees means less dead plant material and fewer nutrients are going into the soil.

Soil and its nutrients are washed by the rain into rivers. Too many nutrients 'pollute' the water by reducing the amount of oxygen and killing off plant and animal species.

Once the fertile topsoil has been washed away, hard layers of soil called <u>laterite</u> increase surface run-off.

Activity

For this activity you will find it useful to refer to the whole of this unit, as well as to your own notes.

You have been asked to record information and some still photographs for a CD-ROM on the Amazon rainforest in Rondonia. The CD is for students aged 12–13, to tell them about what the rainforest is like and how it can be used by people without causing its destruction. The list of possible illustrations (photographs and diagrams) and a short description of what they show is given on the right. Some ideas about what you could record are also given. Write down a transcript of your recorded information for the CD. Organise your transcript under these six headings:

1 What the rainforest looks like, its structure, and its main characteristics.

2 The most important things to understand about a tropical forest ecosystem.

3 The problems that could be created if the rainforest were destroyed **a** locally and **b** globally.

4 The kinds of human activity that can destroy the tropical forest.

5 The ways in which we can learn from traditional farming practices.

6 Suggestions on how a rainforest region such as Rondonia could be managed in a sustainable way.

List of illustrations

- A satellite view of the Amazon forest from space, with the outline of Rondonia's borders marked on it. (Where Rondonia is in the world, in South America, Brazil . . .)
- A picture of rainforest being burned and cut down. (What deforestation is and what causes it.)
- A view of the main road through the rainforest – the Trans-Amazonian Highway – with people travelling along it. (Who is moving into Rondonia, and why.)
- A view of the structure of the rainforest, with emergent trees, canopy and lianas. (What the forest looks like, its climate, weather, etc.)
- A close-up of monkeys, and tree fruits and flowers. (The kind of animals and plants that live in the rainforest. Explain why the forest is important to biodiversity at a world scale.)
- A diagram of the rainforest water cycle. (Explain how the rainforest is important to global weather and climate.)
- A photograph of a Yanomami group 'gardening' in the rainforest. (Find out who the Yanomami are and how they use the rainforest.)
- A picture of land being cleared by a migrant farmer. (Explain how migrant farmers farm the land.)

THINKING GEOGRAPHY

People and environment: the balance of power

In Unit 1 the idea of *environmental determinism* was mentioned. This idea is that the way people live is controlled or determined by the environment in which they live. Here we look at the relationship between people and the planet in a little more depth.

People in charge

Many people now reject the idea of environmental determinism. They argue that humanity has the ability to overcome any of the challenges presented to us by nature. For example, people are able to live in hostile climates such as the deserts of south-west USA. Irrigation schemes such as those in Egypt mean that it is possible to farm in the desert. We are able to control the flow of rivers in order to meet people's needs. Transport links have been built across the most difficult terrains. We have the technology and the ability to control the planet.

The power of nature

The opposing view suggests that despite people's best efforts, the power of the natural forces of our planet means that people will always be at its mercy. Bridges are destroyed by earthquakes, farmland turned into 'desert' by the effects of climatic change. Changes made to the landscape by people are short-lived when compared with the natural processes that have been operating for millions of years.

▼ *The forces of nature.*

▼ *Attempts to control the environment.*
 a *Taking water to the Arizona Desert.*
 b *The Thames Barrier.*
 c *Keeping back the desert sands.*

An alternative view

During the 1980s the Gaia theory became well known. The theory suggests that the welfare of the planet depends on the relationship between the Earth and all its living species.

> 'Within this life realm, every organism is linked, however tenuously, to every other. Microbe, plant and mammal, soil dweller and ocean swimmer, all are caught up in the cycling of energy and nutrients from sun, water, air, and earth.'
>
> From *The Gaia Atlas of Planet Management*, General Editor Norman Byers, published by Gaia Books Ltd, 1984

The theory goes on to suggest that life creates order from the materials around it and that life has the ability to influence the environment. The consequences of such a relationship for the planet Earth are clear. We must be much more careful in the use we make of the planet and the way in which we treat it. The end of the 20th century has seen an increasing awareness of the need to solve global environmental problems before it is too late – too late for the people, that is. The *Earth* will survive, with or without people.

Shades of green

Environmental determinism is an old and simple idea. The question of whether 'the power of nature' is dominant or whether 'people are in charge' is also too simple for the 21st century. The question should be about how people and nature can interact (live together) in a sustainable way. A good definition of sustainability is whether one generation passes on to the next a world that has the same beauty, potential and life-giving qualities as there were in the world they inherited.

The question of sustainability has given birth to green policies. Green politics is about the need for politicians – and others who have to make decisions about the economic and social life of people – to think about the effects of decisions on the environment.

But there are shades of green politics. The 'deep greens' are those who believe human populations must fundamentally change the way in which they live, in order to consume less energy and therefore have less impact on the global climate. People would become closer to nature, understand it better, and stop thinking that they were 'in charge'. This is hard to do when you live in a centrally heated home or drive an air-conditioned car to a climatically controlled shopping mall.

The 'light greens' are those who believe that progress will continue and, as in the past, environmental problems such as pollution will be solved by the application of technology and good management. The 'light greens' may underestimate the seriousness of the environmental crisis.

Activities

1 Skim through this book to find examples where the authors seem to support each of two viewpoints: **a** 'People in charge' and **b** 'The power of nature'.

2 Re-examine Unit 3 Geography and Ecology. People who are said to be 'green' (of whatever shade) usually have an *ecological viewpoint* on anything they study. In one sentence, try to explain what an ecological viewpoint really means. You may want to discuss this with friends first. You might also want to try out your ideas before finally deciding on your sentence.

3 Are you 'dark green', 'light green', or neither of these? Justify your answer.

Landforms, Landscapes and Physical Processes

FOCUS

This unit investigates questions and issues about physical geography and how people interact with the physical world. The main ideas are summarised by the following focus statements:

- There is an interaction between physical processes, landforms and people's activities.

- People have often tried to intervene with physical processes and manage river and coastal environments, with varying degrees of success.

- The drainage basin is an open system in which the flow of water is part of the hydrological cycle.

- Fluvial (water) processes combine with other physical processes (for example weathering) to create river channels and valley landforms.

- Coastal zones undergo constant and often rapid change as a result of the combined effects of physical and human processes.

- Coasts exhibit distinctive landforms.

- Both atmospheric and tectonic processes can result in hazards for people.

- Atmospheric and tectonic processes in combination create the physical landscapes of the world.

To examine these ideas, examples are taken mainly from Britain, but also from Iceland, the Pacific Rim (the Philippines and Japan in particular), North Africa and Europe.

Tectonic activity and its impacts

Earthquakes and volcanoes are spectacular events over which people have very little control. This unit starts by studying Iceland, a country that experiences much volcanic and tectonic activity.

The damage caused by natural hazards depends on the scale of the event and, often, on its location. Earthquakes and volcanic eruptions that occur in densely populated areas usually lead to a greater loss of life than when they occur in remote rural areas. In some ways, volcanic activity can be a positive thing, providing energy to heat homes, and attractions to tourists.

Earth building: a hazardous business

This section describes a **landscape** that has been formed by volcanoes and earthquakes, both products of **tectonic processes**. Both of these events are the result of Iceland's situation on one of the Earth's plate boundaries.

Iceland is a wild and windswept place. The land is bare and there are hardly any trees. Few people live there compared with England. Iceland contains icefields and glaciers, fjords and geysers. There are volcanoes, some of which are still active. Each eruption adds more land to an island that is still being formed.

Figure 4.1

a Volcanic cone. There are many small cinder cones like this one in Iceland. Perhaps this one will grow to be as large as the volcano in the background.

b A recently abandoned fissure now filled by deep water. Molten material once erupted out of this crack in the Earth's crust, and hardened to become basalt. The rock forms most of Iceland.

c Krafla lava field. This is fresh lava from a nearby fissure. Iceland is on an active plate boundary, where new land is being created. The air is heavy with steam and sulphur from the bubbling springs.

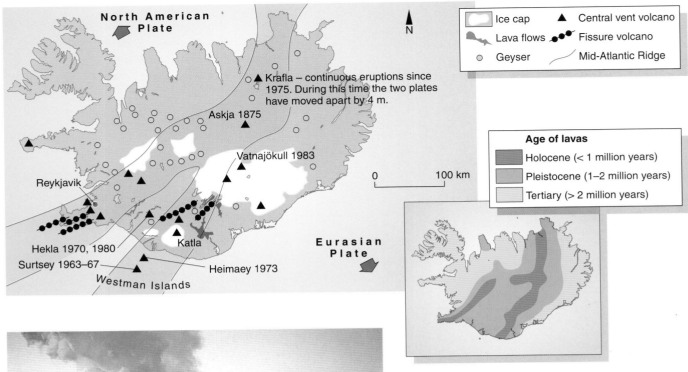

Age of lavas

- Holocene (< 1 million years)
- Pleistocene (1–2 million years)
- Tertiary (> 2 million years)

Ice cap ▲ Central vent volcano
Lava flows ●●● Fissure volcano
○ Geyser Mid-Atlantic Ridge

North American Plate

N

Krafla – continuous eruptions since 1975. During this time the two plates have moved apart by 4 m.

Askja 1875

Vatnajökull 1983

Reykjavik

Hekla 1970, 1980

Katla

Surtsey 1963–67

Heimaey 1973

Westman Islands

Eurasian Plate

0   100 km

▲ **Figure 4.2**
The volcanic features and geological age of Iceland.

◄ **Figure 4.3**
Surtsey. This island near Iceland was formed in 1963 by volcanic eruptions. The volcano used to be on the sea floor but it has built up to become an island.

Activities

1 Iceland is described as 'a wild and windswept place'.

  a Using the photos in **Figure 4.1** to help you, list ten words that accurately describe the scenery.

  b In what ways can volcanic activity be thought of in (i) a positive way and (ii) a negative way?

2 Make a sketch of photograph **4.1b**, and add the following labels: *Vertical cliffs*, *Long thin pool*, *Line of original fissure* (*crack in rock*).

3 Study photograph **4.1c**. What evidence is there that this is a newly formed landscape?

Extension activity

4 Explain how you can trace the line of active volcanoes and earthquakes from the ages of rocks (**Figure 4.2**).

5 'Iceland is a country that is still being formed.' Write 200 words to back up this statement, making use of **Figures 4.1–4.3**.

The movement of the Earth's plates

To find out why there are volcanoes and earthquakes in Iceland, we need to investigate how and why the Earth's plates move. Plates are gigantic, slow-moving slabs of the Earth's crust. Some plates are topped with continental landmass, while others are completely made up of ocean floor. The plates are driven by powerful convection movements of material in the mantle below the crust. It is plate movement that causes earthquakes and volcanoes (Figure 4.4).

Figure 4.5 shows that plate movement is the result of slow currents of material called **magma** in the asthenosphere underneath the plates. Some parts of the molten mass are hotter than others. Where it is hottest, there is a slow-moving plume of magma rising underneath the plates. Where the magma is coolest it sinks deeper into the Earth's interior. It is this movement of magma that drags and moves the plates above.

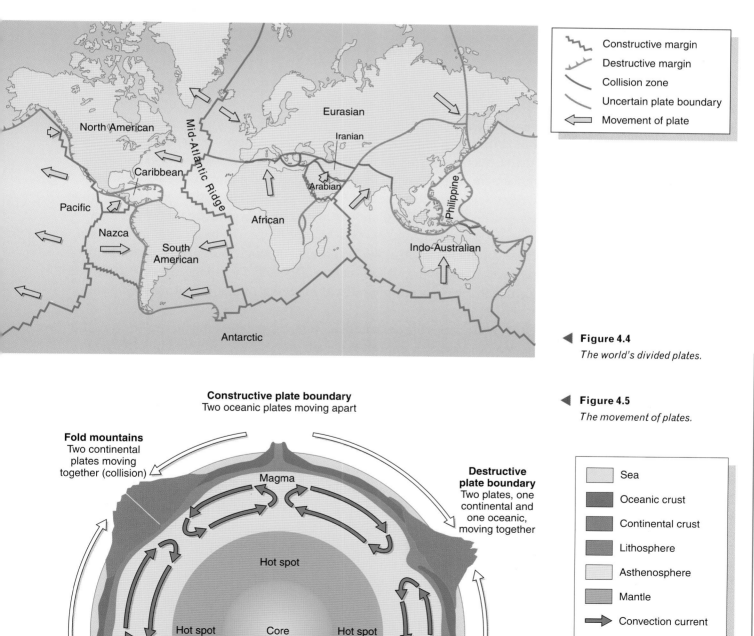

◀ **Figure 4.4**
The world's divided plates.

◀ **Figure 4.5**
The movement of plates.

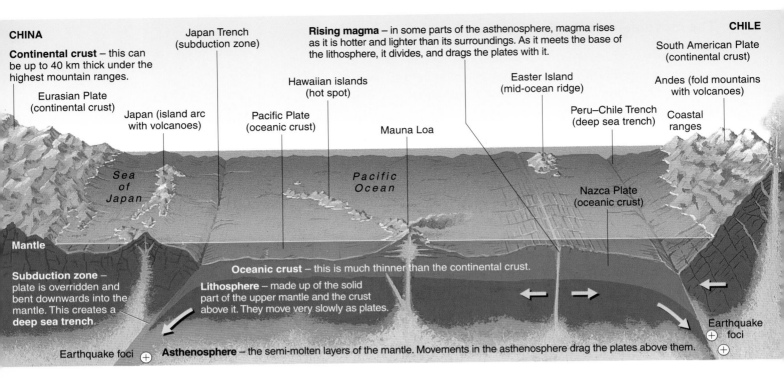

CHINA

Continental crust – this can be up to 40 km thick under the highest mountain ranges.

Eurasian Plate (continental crust)

Japan (island arc with volcanoes)

Sea of Japan

Japan Trench (subduction zone)

Pacific Plate (oceanic crust)

Hawaiian islands (hot spot)

Mauna Loa

Pacific Ocean

Rising magma – in some parts of the asthenosphere, magma rises as it is hotter and lighter than its surroundings. As it meets the base of the lithosphere, it divides, and drags the plates with it.

Easter Island (mid-ocean ridge)

CHILE

South American Plate (continental crust)

Andes (fold mountains with volcanoes)

Peru–Chile Trench (deep sea trench)

Coastal ranges

Nazca Plate (oceanic crust)

Mantle

Subduction zone – plate is overridden and bent downwards into the mantle. This creates a **deep sea trench**.

Oceanic crust – this is much thinner than the continental crust.

Lithosphere – made up of the solid part of the upper mantle and the crust above it. They move very slowly as plates.

Earthquake foci ⊕

Asthenosphere – the semi-molten layers of the mantle. Movements in the asthenosphere drag the plates above them.

Earthquake foci ⊕ ⊕

▲ **Figure 4.6**
Plate tectonics in the Pacific Ocean.

At some plate boundaries the Earth's crust is being forced apart to form **constructive** plate margins. Here, new land is being formed, made of rocks from inside the Earth. These are igneous rocks, meaning that they were molten at first, but have since cooled to become solid. Figure 4.6 shows plate movements in the Pacific Ocean. There are similar movements in the Atlantic Ocean. Scientists calculate that America moves 2 cm further away from Europe every year, and that the Atlantic grows wider. The ocean bed gets older with increasing distance from the Mid-Atlantic Ridge. The basalt near the coasts of these continents is 200 million years old. Although most of this ridge is below sea level, it passes through the centre of Iceland. In geological terms, rocks formed in the Holocene period (within the last million years) are very recent.

Other boundaries are **destructive**. Here, crustal material disappears into the mantle. This is not a smooth and even process. It is jerky and involves huge force, which also results in volcanoes and earthquakes.

Plate movements and the formation of fold mountains

The world's highest mountains have been created by plate movements (Figure 4.7). For example, 100 million years ago, the Indian Plate started to converge with the Eurasian Plate. Gradually the ocean between them narrowed until the two continental landmasses collided. Between the two continents were thick layers of deposits carried into the sea by rivers which had eroded the land. As the plates collided, these sediments were squeezed and folded to form the Himalayas. The process continues today, with the Indian Plate grinding under the Eurasian Plate at a rate of 5 cm a year.

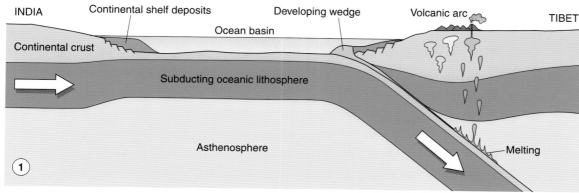

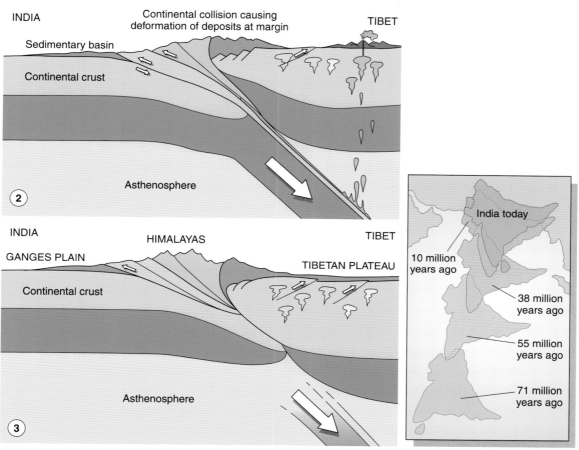

Figure 4.7

Stages in the formation of the Himalayas.

(Within image 2, stage 1)
INDIA — Continental shelf deposits — Developing wedge — Volcanic arc — TIBET
Ocean basin
Continental crust
Subducting oceanic lithosphere
Asthenosphere
Melting
①

(Within image 1, stage 2)
INDIA — Continental collision causing deformation of deposits at margin — TIBET
Sedimentary basin
Continental crust
Asthenosphere
②

(Stage 3)
INDIA — HIMALAYAS — TIBET
GANGES PLAIN — TIBETAN PLATEAU
Continental crust
Asthenosphere
③

(Inset map)
India today
10 million years ago
38 million years ago
55 million years ago
71 million years ago

Activities

1 Write a short explanation of the following terms:
 plates
 constructive plate boundary
 destructive plate boundary
 magma
 crust
 ocean trench
 subduction zone
 fold mountains

2 Describe how magma moves in the Earth's mantle and how this affects plate movement.

3 With the help of diagrams, describe the processes that occur at:
 a destructive plate boundaries
 b constructive plate boundaries.

4 Using **Figure 4.6** suggest how the Hawaiian island chain is evidence that plates have moved huge distances.

5 Use the information in **Figure 4.7** to explain how fold mountains are the result of converging plates.

6 a What is the evidence which suggests that Europe and Africa were once joined to North and South America? (See **Figure 4.4**.)

 b What further evidence would you suggest scientists could look for?

Why do earthquakes happen?

Earthquakes are shock waves resulting from sudden movements in the Earth's crust. They usually occur near plate boundaries. This section describes how earthquakes are caused, and explains why they can be so damaging. The case study of the 1995 Kobe earthquake in Japan shows how serious the effects of earthquakes can be.

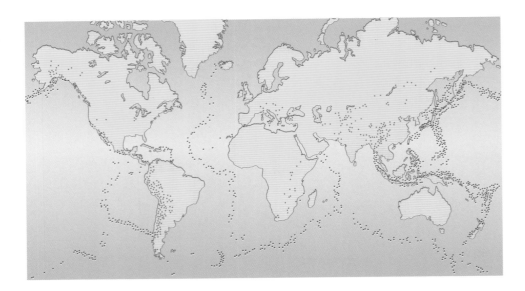

Earthquakes occur near plate boundaries and volcanoes. The huge masses of rock that make up plates do not move smoothly past each other. Instead, stress builds up as the rocks are locked together. At first rocks deform and bend as the pressure mounts. Eventually, they reach their breaking point and the rocks move to adjust to the pressure. This is called **strain**. There are lines of weakness, called **faults**, where rocks have given way before and are likely to do so again. Earthquakes are the result of shock waves from this sudden movement. The greater the pressure that builds up, the greater the vibrations that are sent out when the rocks suddenly 'snap', or shift.

▶ **Figure 4.9**

Earthquake focus and epicentre. The focus marks the point of sudden movement. The epicentre is the point on the ground surface directly above the focus where the shock waves first arrive and are at their most powerful. They gradually reduce with distance away from this point until they become harmless.

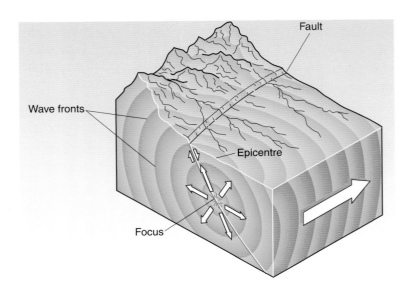

Year	Place	No. of deaths	Richter scale	Effects
1906	San Francisco, California	1,500	8.1–8.2	Fires caused extensive damage
1908	Messina, Italy	120,000		
1920	Kansu, China	180,000		
1923	Tokyo, Japan	143,000	7.9	Fire caused extensive destruction
1960	Southern Chile	5,700	8.5–8.6	Possibly the largest-magnitude earthquake ever recorded
1964	Alaska	131	8.3–8.4	
1970	Peru	66,000	7.8	Great rockslide
1971	San Fernando, California	65	6.5	Damage exceeded $1 billion
1975	Liaoning Province, China	Few	7.5	First major earthquake to be predicted
1976	Tangshan, China	240,000	7.6	Not predicted
1985	Mexico City	9,500	8.1	Major damage occurred 400 km from epicentre
1988	Soviet Armenia	25,000	6.9	Poor construction practices contributed to destruction
1989	San Francisco Bay area	62	7.1	Damage exceeded $6 billion
1990	North-west Iran	50,000	7.3	Landslides and poor construction caused great damage
1992	Cairo, Egypt	500	5.9	
1993	Latur, India	10,000	6.5	Poor construction practices caused great damage and loss of life
1995	Kobe, Japan	5,477	7.2	

◀ **Figure 4.10**

Notable earthquakes in the 20th century.

Activities

1 What is an earthquake?

2 Explain why most earthquakes occur at plate boundaries.

3 Using information in **Figure 4.10**, draw a graph to compare the number of deaths with earthquake magnitude. Does your graph show a simple relationship?

Disaster in Kobe: a case study for you to write

The newspaper cuttings in Figure 4.11 give information about the earthquake that devastated the city of Kobe in Japan in 1995. There is also information taken from a website on the Internet based in Kobe. Your task is to write an account of the earthquake, its causes and effects. You should begin by making notes under the following headings:

1 Describe what happened. Try to include facts and figures about the damage. Use quotes from eye-witnesses.

2 Using diagrams and writing, explain why the earthquake happened.

3 Describe what has happened in Kobe since the first 'quake. What problems did the city and country have? What help did they receive? How is reconstruction proceeding?

'Books went flying and the room shook like a jelly'

BY RAYMOND WHITAKER

Michael Miller woke at quarter to six yesterday morning to find his room, high over the city of Kobe, "shaking like a jelly".

Books were cascading from shelves, furniture falling over and objects as heavy as refrigerators sliding around as though on a skating rink. "It took me several seconds to realise what was going on," said Dr. Miller, dean of the Kobe Institute, "but I and all the students managed to get out unscathed. It was a miracle no one was hurt, when people a quarter of a mile away were killed."

Figure 4.11

The Kobe earthquake.

a *Newspaper extracts from the* Independent, *18–19 January 1995.*

b *From the Internet.*

a

Thousands flee ruins of Japanese quake city

FROM ABI SEKIMITSU
of Reuter and agencies

Kobe – Hundreds of thousands of people fled Kobe yesterday, abandoning the smouldering ruins of a city in which over 3,000 are now known to have died. As darkness fell for the second time since the earthquake struck, more than 800 people were still missing, presumed buried in the rubble.

This morning, a major fire broke out in the main shopping area of the city. The new fire came after a huge explosion at 7.30am. Lack of firefighting water, a strong northerly wind and extremely dry conditions meant the fire could spread to other large department stores nearby.

On foot, by bicycle, in shared cars, the survivors packed the main roads out of town. Some were limping, others in bandages, looking like war refugees as they picked their way past collapsed buildings. Only lines of hearses were heading into town.

Rescue workers worked into the darkness to recover more bodies. Many of the victims were found in the beds or futons (floor mattresses) in which they had been sleeping when the quake struck at 5.45am on Tuesday.

b

Why the earthquake happened

The focus of the Kobe earthquake is calculated to be almost directly underneath the city at a depth of around 30 km (18 miles). It happened on a minor geological fault that lies above the zone where the Pacific and Philippine tectonic plates collide with the Eurasian plate and fold underneath it, making the area prone to earthquakes.

The same processes which caused the earthquake were responsible for the creation of the Japanese islands: as the rock descended below the Eurasian plate it melted and rose to the surface as volcanic lava creating a string of islands.

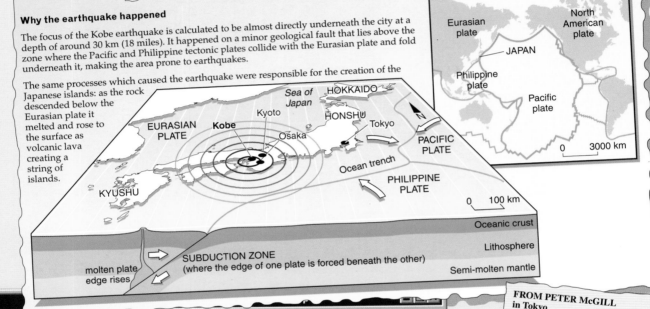

FROM PETER McGILL
in Tokyo

The most devastating earthquake to strike a Japanese city in 70 years left more than 1,800 confirmed dead last night and 1,000 missing, believed trapped under the rubble.

Twenty-four hours after the quake, which measured 7.2 on the Richter scale, the sky above the port of Kobe was still crimson with flame. Efforts to control 150 fires were hampered by shattered water mains. Authorities were planning to use helicopters today to bomb the fires with water from Osaka Bay.

As night fell, and criticism grew of the slowness of the official response, rescuers dug through rubble with their bare hands. "We are still calling out to people in case they are trapped. But we are getting fewer and fewer answers," one rescue official said. "We just keep calling out . . . What else can we do." It was reported that 45 people had been pulled from the rubble of a collapsed hospital.

The scale of the disaster stunned a country which regarded itself as better defended against earthquakes than other nations.

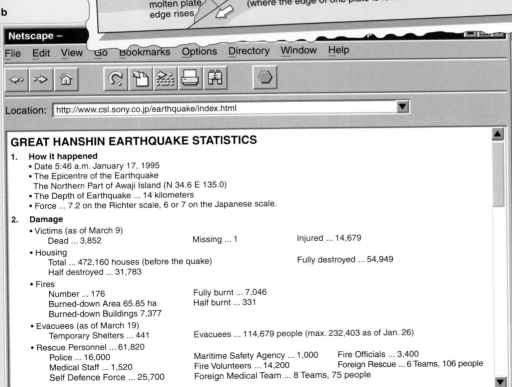

Netscape –

File   Edit   View   Go   Bookmarks   Options   Directory   Window   Help

Location: http://www.csl.sony.co.jp/earthquake/index.html

GREAT HANSHIN EARTHQUAKE STATISTICS

1. **How it happened**
   - Date 5:46 a.m. January 17, 1995
   - The Epicentre of the Earthquake
     The Northern Part of Awaji Island (N 34.6 E 135.0)
   - The Depth of Earthquake ... 14 kilometers
   - Force ... 7.2 on the Richter scale, 6 or 7 on the Japanese scale.

2. **Damage**
   - Victims (as of March 9)

Dead ... 3,852	Missing ... 1	Injured ... 14,679

   - Housing

Total ... 472,160 houses (before the quake)	Fully destroyed ... 54,949
Half destroyed ... 31,783	

   - Fires

Number ... 176	Fully burnt ... 7,046
Burned-down Area 65.85 ha	Half burnt ... 331
Burned-down Buildings 7,377	

   - Evacuees (as of March 19)

Temporary Shelters ... 441	Evacuees ... 114,679 people (max. 232,403 as of Jan. 26)

   - Rescue Personnel ... 61,820

Police ... 16,000	Maritime Safety Agency ... 1,000	Fire Officials ... 3,400
Medical Staff ... 1,520	Fire Volunteers ... 14,200	Foreign Rescue ... 6 Teams, 106 people
Self Defence Force ... 25,700	Foreign Medical Team ... 8 Teams, 75 people	

The Internet

Your teacher may have a list of useful websites. You can use the Internet to search for information on a subject of topical geographical interest.

- Write a report on what you discover from the Internet.
- What do you think are the problems of using information from the Internet?

(*Hint:* Who writes it? What for? Is there any editor or publisher as there is for a newspaper or book?)

Geographical information systems

Geographical information systems, or GIS, can be described as 'intelligent maps'. They are computer programs that store information about an area, and can produce maps with one or more layers of data at a time. Many cities in the UK use GIS to keep track of things like cable TV networks, gas pipelines, and so on.

The maps in Figure 4.12 were produced using a CD-ROM containing a GIS of the world. They show the main Japanese island of Honshu. Map A has only two layers – oceans and coastline. Map B also has the height of the land split into layers. Map C shows urban areas, motorways, and multiple-track railways (the last two are not easy to distinguish at this scale).

- How do you think city planners in Kobe could use GIS to help in the reconstruction of their city?

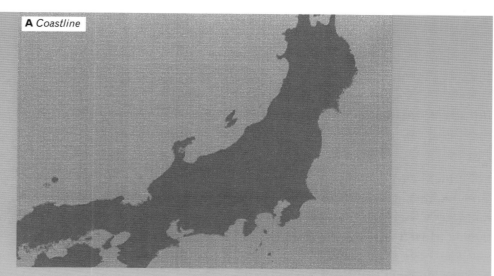

A *Coastline*

Figure 4.12
GIS maps of Japan.

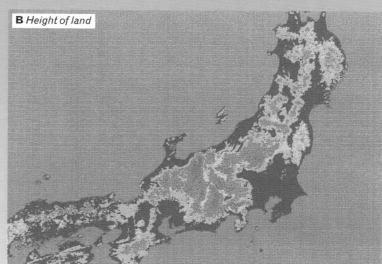

B *Height of land*

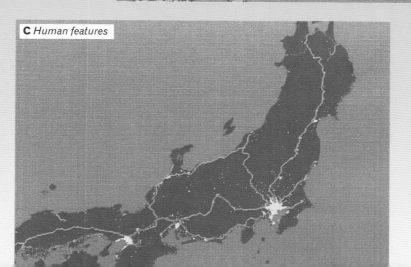

C *Human features*

Volcanoes

The violence of a volcanic eruption is related to the type of lava (magma which reaches the Earth's surface) that spills onto the surface. Runny lava flows freely, forming 'shield' volcanoes such as those that make Hawaii. Thick, stiffer lava can be more explosive. The 1991 Mount Pinatubo eruption in the Philippines was characteristic of an explosive volcano near to a destructive plate boundary. These days, scientists are getting better at predicting the behaviour of volcanoes and the date of their eruptions.

Mount Pinatubo: a case study

Mount Pinatubo is on Luzon, one of the largest islands in the Philippines. The eruption in 1991 was the largest for 80 years. This case study shows how scientists monitored the build-up of the magma and were able to predict when it would erupt.

Arriving in the Philippines

Darkness in daytime, ash from the sky, and a trembling ground of repeated earthquakes. 'It was like the end of the world,' my taxi-driver said. The headlights glared off the wet pavement ahead, picking out the silhouettes of grey, ash-covered pedestrians. I had come to the Philippines to see an erupting volcano, but the explosions from Mount Pinatubo were 90 km north-west of the capital. The weather overhead was a combination of tropical storms and huge amounts of tiny volcanic material suspended in the air. I was seeing the result of the most powerful eruption in the last 80 years.

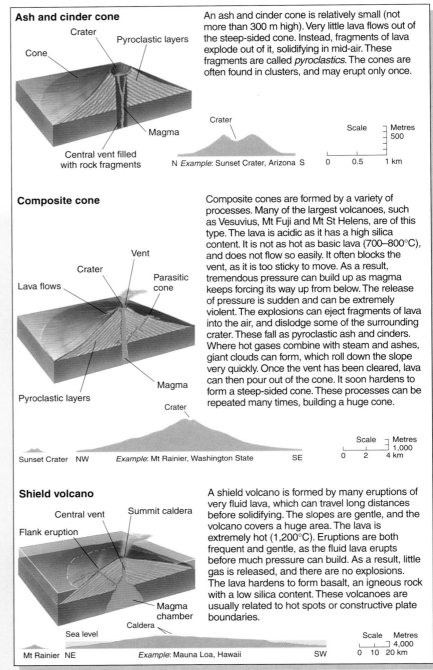

Ash and cinder cone

An ash and cinder cone is relatively small (not more than 300 m high). Very little lava flows out of the steep-sided cone. Instead, fragments of lava explode out of it, solidifying in mid-air. These fragments are called *pyroclastics*. The cones are often found in clusters, and may erupt only once.

Example: Sunset Crater, Arizona

Composite cone

Composite cones are formed by a variety of processes. Many of the largest volcanoes, such as Vesuvius, Mt Fuji and Mt St Helens, are of this type. The lava is acidic as it has a high silica content. It is not as hot as basic lava (700–800°C), and does not flow so easily. It often blocks the vent, as it is too sticky to move. As a result, tremendous pressure can build up as magma keeps forcing its way up from below. The release of pressure is sudden and can be extremely violent. The explosions can eject fragments of lava into the air, and dislodge some of the surrounding crater. These fall as pyroclastic ash and cinders. Where hot gases combine with steam and ashes, giant clouds can form, which roll down the slope very quickly. Once the vent has been cleared, lava can then pour out of the cone. It soon hardens to form a steep-sided cone. These processes can be repeated many times, building a huge cone.

Example: Mt Rainier, Washington State

Shield volcano

A shield volcano is formed by many eruptions of very fluid lava, which can travel long distances before solidifying. The slopes are gentle, and the volcano covers a huge area. The lava is extremely hot (1,200°C). Eruptions are both frequent and gentle, as the fluid lava erupts before much pressure can build. As a result, little gas is released, and there are no explosions. The lava hardens to form basalt, an igneous rock with a low silica content. These volcanoes are usually related to hot spots or constructive plate boundaries.

Example: Mauna Loa, Hawaii

The eruption

The eruption of Mount Pinatubo on 15 June 1991 sent 6 cubic kilometres of ash into the atmosphere; 40,500 hectares of surrounding countryside were covered with a blanket of ash; 650,000 people lost their jobs; 110,000 homes were destroyed; 200,000 people were moved to refugee camps; and 1,000 people died as a result of the eruption.

Lives saved!

The death toll was relatively low, as a result of improved technology in understanding and monitoring volcanic behaviour. American scientists at the nearby Clark airforce base installed equipment in the mountainside

Figure 4.14
The location of Mount Pinatubo.

when the first rumblings began in April. Seismometers measured small earthquakes caused by magma forcing its way up to the chamber below the volcano. The earthquakes were spread over an area of 6 square kilometres, suggesting that there was a large amount of magma under the surface. Tiltmeters recorded changes in slope gradient, as the volcano started to bulge. Air samples were taken from the regular helicopter surveys of the mountain. Scientists noted the high level of sulphur dioxide in the air, a sure sign of a forthcoming eruption.

Disaster warning!

The scientists were both excited and anxious. The lava from this eruption would be very viscous (thick) and unlikely to flow freely. As a result, the scientists expected that most material would be ejected in the form of ash, steam and gases. A study of the layers of ash showed that there had been only five eruptions in the last 2,000 years. All the signs were that this was going to be an eruption of enormous power.

Figure 4.15
The eruption of Mount Pinatubo, 1991.

The scientists were expected to give warnings as the date of the eruption approached, but it was difficult for them to give exact predictions. They hesitated in declaring a level 3 state of alert – this would mean that the eruption would be within a fortnight. It would lead to the evacuation of the area around the volcano. This could cause panic as thousands of villagers left their farms. The airforce base would need to evacuate

both its staff and the expensive aircraft and equipment there. The scientists would lose credibility if they were wrong, but they declared a level 3 alert on 6 June. Two days later, the highest level of alert – level 4 – was announced, meaning that the eruption was likely within 48 hours. At that point, 120,000 people who lived within 20 km of Pinatubo fled for safety.

The aftermath

The first eruption was on 10 June, but that just unblocked the vent. At dawn on 15 June a huge blast blew out the side of the mountain. By 2 pm the sky was black with ash and falling chunks of pumice. Deadly clouds of superheated gases and pyroclastic fragments rolled down the volcano's slopes at speeds of 120 km per hour. An estimated 20 million tonnes of sulphur dioxide rose 40 km into the upper atmosphere. The eruption continued until September.

The main danger during the eruption was from **lahars** – rapidly moving torrents of liquefied ash and mud which funnel down valleys. The unstable volcanic deposits are turned into this cement-like slurry after heavy rain. The rainy season will continue to bring the deadly threat of lahars for many years. The huge mass of tiny sulphur and dust particles spread over the Earth's upper atmosphere, blocking out 2 per cent of incoming sunlight. Meteorologists believe this affected weather patterns all over the world.

Activities

1 Write a short explanation, or definition, of the following terms:
 vent
 crater
 lava flow
 cone
 parasitic cone
 magma chamber.

2 Why are most volcanoes close to plate boundaries?

3 Produce a table comparing three types of volcano. Using **Figure 4.13**, you should compare:
 • the size of the cone
 • the frequency and violence of the eruptions
 • the type of material ejected
 • the characteristics of the lava.

4 a List the main causes of death and destruction from the Pinatubo eruption.

 b What are lahars? Why will they continue to be a danger for a long time?

5 a Explain how scientists monitored the build-up to the eruption of 15 June.

 b The experts were very worried that their predictions would not be exactly right, because they would 'lose credibility'. From the point of view of local people, why is it so important that disaster warnings are correct?

Coasts – the processes of erosion, transportation and deposition

Physical processes shape the coast. Coastlines are where land, water and air meet. They are dynamic, and capable of rapid change.

Thousands of sightseers poured into Scarborough in June 1993 to see the £1 million Holbeck Hall plunge into the sea. The four-star hotel became the east coast's biggest tourist attraction when it was left teetering 45 metres above sea level by a landslip. David Jacobs, who lives nearby, said: 'I was in tears. The noise was like a ship going down, timbers creaking, glass and masonry breaking. It was eerie.' Joan Turner, who owns the hotel, added: 'We evacuated the place very quickly. It's a tremendous relief no-one was hurt. We can't build the hotel up again – there's nothing to build it on.'

Why did Holbeck Hall go?

Waves are caused by the action of wind blowing over the surface of the sea. The tugging of the wind on the surface causes a wave to form. The wave moves *through* the water, but the water itself does not move forward – a bit like the wave you make when you shake a rope. The wave-shape moves along the rope, but the rope itself does not move along. The height and strength of the wave depend on wind speed and the distance a wave has travelled. The greater the wind speed and distance, or **fetch**, the higher the wave and the greater its energy. Waves 'break' when they enter shallow coastal waters and meet the friction of the seashore. When a wave breaks, energy is released and the water moves forward.

The way waves break determines whether they are constructive or destructive. **Constructive** waves have low energy. They deposit materials and build beaches. **Destructive** waves have more energy and can remove the sand from a beach very quickly. The most destructive waves occur during storms – it is then that the erosive power of waves is at its greatest. Figure 4.17 shows the different effects of breaking waves.

There are four distinct coastal erosion processes:

- **Hydraulic action** Air trapped in cracks in the rock 'explodes' when put under pressure from advancing waves.

- **Corrasion** Waves hurl particles at cliff surfaces.

- **Attrition** The particles themselves are broken down as they rub against one another and against the cliff face.

- **Corrosion** The chemical decomposition of rock by sea water.

▲ **Figure 4.16**
Cliffhanger: doomed Holbeck clings to the precipice.

▼ **Figure 4.17**
Constructive and destructive waves.

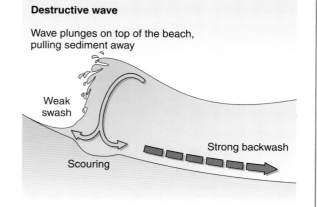

Constructive wave

Wave crest breaks and advances, pushing sediment up the beach

Strong swash

Weak backwash

Destructive wave

Wave plunges on top of the beach, pulling sediment away

Weak swash

Strong backwash

Scouring

Mass movement on slopes

The stability of a slope depends on how well it can resist the force of gravity pulling it down. Resistance depends mainly on the cohesion of the slope material. Normally a slope finds an equilibrium – just the right angle for all the conditions. The processes of mass movement, like soil creep, happen all the time, but they are usually slow. However, mass movement can also happen quickly – as in a landslide or a slump – when the normal conditions are upset. For example, cohesion can be reduced when the slope material is saturated with water. Or the slope angle can be increased by undercutting. Waves often undercut slopes at the coast, creating very steep slopes (cliffs).

Andrew Blackler, a geographer from Reading University, blames heavy rain in the spring of 1991, following several dry summers, for the landslip at Holbeck Hall. 'The drying and shrinking of the clay caused cracks to appear, which were then filled with water. The pressure of the hotel and the swimming-pool, wouldn't have helped, either.'

The East Yorkshire coast, with its steep but soft clay cliffs, has always been vulnerable. South of Scarborough, the 65-km stretch of Holderness is the fastest-eroding coastline in Europe. It is constantly undercut by attacking waves, and retreats at an average of 2 metres per year.

Waves can create certain **erosional** landforms such as cliffs, caves, stacks and stumps. They can also transport material and deposit it to form **depositional** landforms, such as beaches.

Activities

1 State two sources of sediment in the coastal system.

2 Describe two coastal landforms created by erosion and two created by deposition.

3 Describe how sediment is carried by wave energy from where it is eroded to where it is deposited.

4 Explain how a reduction in the rates of erosion along one part of a coastline may mean less deposition in another.

5 Using all the evidence in this section, finish off the newspaper article in **Figure 4.16** by explaining the processes that *caused* the landslip at Holbeck Hall.

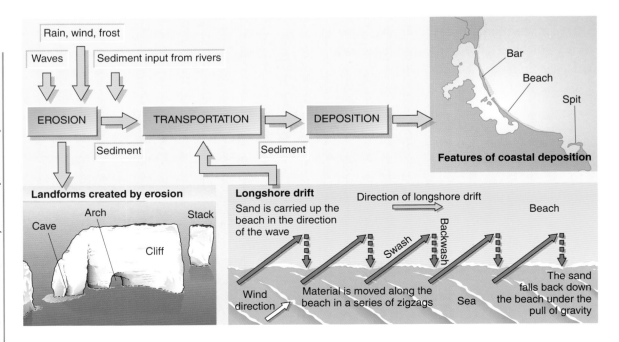

◀ **Figure 4.18**
The coastal system.

The impact of people on the coast: a case study

On a field trip to the north Norfolk coast, GCSE students investigated the impact of human activity on the coast. They first collected some background information on the issues facing this stretch of coastline. Their enquiry was concerned with coastal protection, to identify the best ways to stop coastlines being eroded.

◀ **Figure 4.19**
Extract from OS 1:50 000 map sheet 133.

▼ **Figure 4.20**
Geological map of north Norfolk.

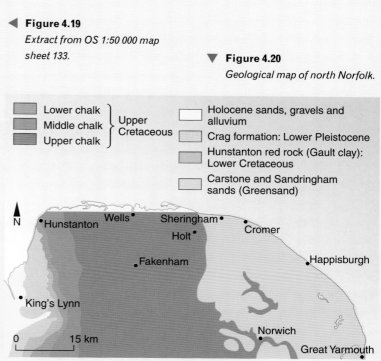

The study area is located on deposits called 'Crag formation'. This is a mixture of sands, gravels and shelly fragments held together by clay. The cliffs are also very porous and quickly become saturated with water. As a result, rapid mass movements including mudflows are very common in this area (Figure 4.22).

Weathering is when rocks are broken down by exposure to air, water and changing temperatures.

Erosion is when the Earth's surface is shaped by the action of moving agents such as water, wind and ice. Material is worn away and then removed by these agents.

Sea walls are the most effective means of preventing erosion, but they are also the most expensive. Even with a sea wall, engineers now recognise that the beach is the best coast protection. Where waves erode the beach material, they can also undermine the sea wall. Groynes are needed to hold the beach in place.

Unit 4 Landforms, Landscapes and Physical Processes

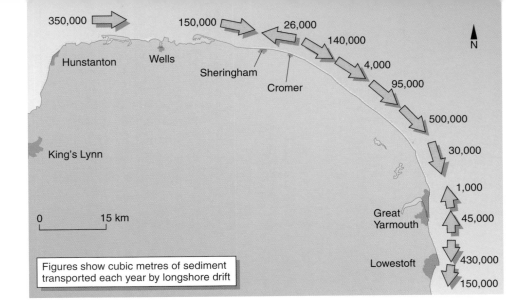

▶ **Figure 4.21**
Sediment flows and rates of erosion along the East Anglian coast.

350,000

150,000

26,000

140,000

4,000

95,000

500,000

30,000

1,000

45,000

430,000

150,000

Hunstanton

Wells

Sheringham

Cromer

King's Lynn

Great Yarmouth

Lowestoft

N

0   15 km

Figures show cubic metres of sediment transported each year by longshore drift

▼ **Figure 4.22**
Field trip to Norfolk.

a *Standing on a mudflow near East Runton Gap.*

b *Sea wall defences at Sheringham.*

The students from Acland Burghley school interviewed local people in Sheringham. They found that coastal erosion was a controversial issue for a number of reasons.

- It is very expensive. For example, it cost £134,000 to repair recent storm damage to the sea defences at Sheringham.

- It can look unsightly.

- If coastal erosion is prevented in one place, erosion problems can actually increase further along the coast.

- There is a lot of debate about who should pay for coastal protection. Should it be the taxpayer? If so, what about those people who don't live near the sea?

Activities

1 Using **Figure 4.19**, draw your own land use map of the coastal area with the following land use categories:
   - urban areas
   - roads
   - railways
   - leisure facilities
   - agricultural land

   Include as many different coastal features as you can.

2 What evidence is there on the map to indicate that erosion is happening along this stretch of the coast? Mark these places on your map.

3 What evidence is there on the map that people have tried to protect the coast from erosion? Mark examples on your map.

4 Is there any relationship between the type of land use and where the coast protection measures have been used?

a

Revetments are used where the expense of a sea wall cannot be justified. They break the force of the waves and trap beach material behind them to protect the base of the cliffs. But they do not give total protection to the cliff foot as a sea wall does. Groynes can be used to stop the waves undermining the revetment.

Rip-rap (concrete blocks) help to protect the base of the cliffs by breaking up the waves' energy

Steel piling used to hold the rip-rap in place

b

The interruption of longshore drift by groynes can starve beaches further along the coast where erosion may also be a problem

Groynes interrupt the pattern of longshore drift. Material accumulates on the up-drift side, building up the beach. A wide beach is a good form of protection against cliff erosion. It also has benefits for tourism.

c

Storm ridge

▲ **Figure 4.23**
The three sites where students collected beach profile information.

▶ **Figure 4.24**
Data for three beach profiles on the north Norfolk coast.

Site 1: grid reference 248412			Site 2: grid reference 228421			Site 3: grid reference 150436		
Distance* (metres)	Angle*	Average shingle size	Distance* (metres)	Angle*	Average shingle size	Distance* (metres)	Angle*	Average shingle size
54	8	2.95 cm	60	2	3.12 cm	13	13	6.00 cm
2.4	41		46	4		3.8	14	
12.5	6		30	3		5.8	12	
Cliff	43		Cliff	34		3.3	20	
						6	7	
						6.2	5	
						Cliff	59	

*The profile was measured from the water line. Each length represents the distance between one break of slope and the next.

Activities

1 Match the data and grid references in **Figure 4.24** with **Figure 4.19**, and with each of the photographs in **Figure 4.23**.

2 Which of the sites have been the most managed (changed or influenced in some way by people) and the least managed? Explain your answer using **Figures 4.19, 4.23** and **4.24**.

3 a What different methods have been used to protect parts of the north Norfolk coast?
 b Explain how each of these methods works.

4 What has been the impact of management on the beach profiles? You will need to think about:
 • the angles of the cliff and beaches
 • the length of the beach
 • the size of beach material.

5 Choose three methods of coastal protection. What are the costs and benefits of each method in the shorter term (up to 5 years) and the longer term (20–30 years)? Your answer could be written in three tables, each set out like the one below.

Method:	Costs	Benefits
• Shorter term		
• Longer term		

The work of rivers – erosion, transportation and deposition

The water in a river is capable of wearing away or eroding the channel in which it flows. This happens when the water is in motion. The faster or more turbulent the movement, the greater the potential for erosion. Rivers with a large discharge or steep gradient erode because:

- the river has great potential energy and a high velocity

- the water moves in a turbulent fashion.

The amount of erosion also depends on the strength and make-up of the material over which the river flows. Figure 4.25 shows that coarse sand can be eroded more easily than any other size of particle. Small clay particles tend to stick together, while pebbles, stones and boulders are much heavier.

There are four main processes of river erosion, matching very closely the processes of coastal erosion (see page 101):

- **Corrasion** Material being carried by the river is thrown against its bed and banks.

- **Attrition** Particles being carried are thrown against each other, resulting in smaller and more rounded fragments.

- **Hydraulic action** The actual force of the turbulent water can dislodge material.

- **Corrosion** Water dissolves particles and carries them in solution.

▶ **Figure 4.25**

Relationship between river velocity and particle size.

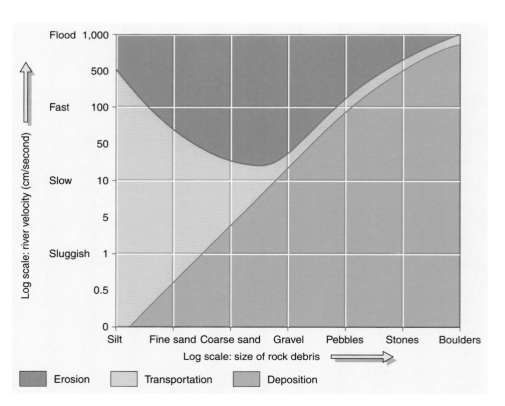

Sediment can be carried by a river, especially when it is in flood, until it lacks the energy to take it any further. The heavier particles are either rolled along the bottom or 'hop' with the turbulent flow of the water (this is called **saltation**), while the lighter particles are carried much further in suspension. Dissolved material is transported in solution by rivers even at their lowest flow.

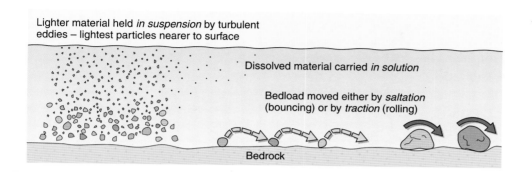

Lighter material held *in suspension* by turbulent eddies – lightest particles nearer to surface

Dissolved material carried *in solution*

Bedload moved either by *saltation* (bouncing) or by *traction* (rolling)

Bedrock

◀ **Figure 4.26**
River transportation of sediments.

The river Dee: a case study

The river Dee has its source to the south-east of Snowdonia National Park. It flows east through the hills of central north Wales, before turning northwards on the Welsh–English border. It then flows through Chester to its mouth at Connah's Quay. The river is about 150 km long.

▶ **Figure 4.27**
The river Dee.

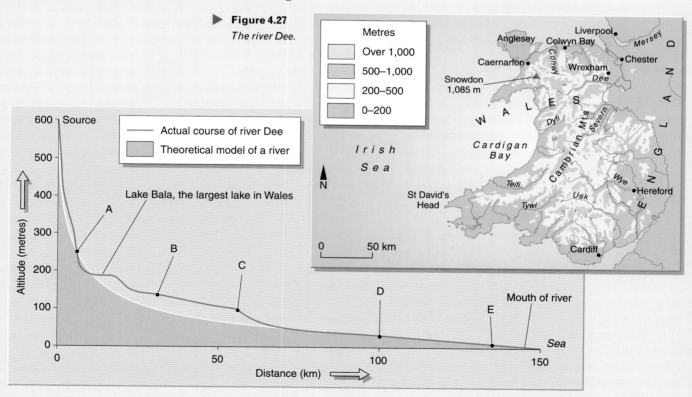

The gradient of the river is steep at first, but soon becomes more gentle and almost horizontal as it nears the sea. The sea is at **base level**, the lowest level to which a river can erode.

▲ **Figure 4.28**
The long profile of the river Dee, and the theoretical model of a river.

The upper course

The streams begin high on the side of a mountain. They lose height very quickly at first. Several small tributaries meet to become a fast-flowing stream. The stream has eroded downwards to form a deep V-shaped valley. The slopes rise directly from the side of the stream (Figure 4.29). The steep land is used for grazing sheep. Other headwater valleys are forested. The V-shaped valley is a result of river erosion and mass movement (see page 102) on the hillside. As the river undercuts its banks it makes the slopes steeper until they become unstable and unable to support their own weight. This causes landslips which bring loose material down to the valley bottom.

The middle course

The gradient is much gentler, and the channel meanders across the width of its floodplain (Figure 4.30). Meanders are formed by the river eroding and depositing sediment on the flood plain. The river is deeper and has more energy on the outside of a curve. There is enough energy to erode the outside bank, forming a small cliff. The river undercuts the bank, sometimes causing it to collapse. It is shallower on the inside of the curve where the river drops some of its load to form **point bars**.

When the river channel is full the river is said to be **in flood**. It has a lot of energy, which means that it can carry large amounts of sediment. Occasionally the river overflows its main channel or bed, and the water loses speed as it spreads out over the floodplain. The floodwater deposits a layer of silt particles on the valley floor. This process has been repeated many times to give fertile, moist land. It provides ideal grazing land for cattle, but is very dangerous land on which to build. The settlements and roads are on the valley side, above the area that is at risk from flooding.

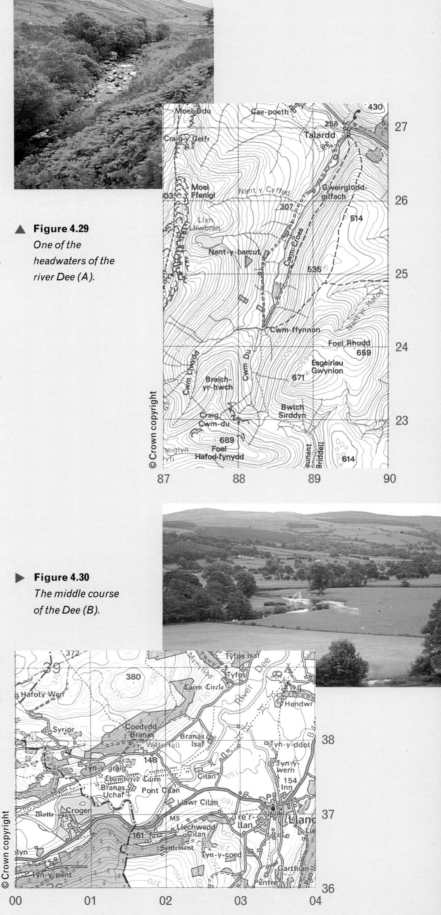

▲ **Figure 4.29**
One of the headwaters of the river Dee (A).

© Crown copyright

▶ **Figure 4.30**
The middle course of the Dee (B).

© Crown copyright

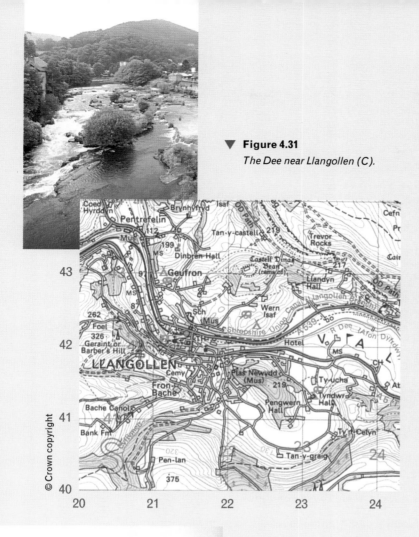

Figure 4.31
The Dee near Llangollen (C).

© Crown copyright

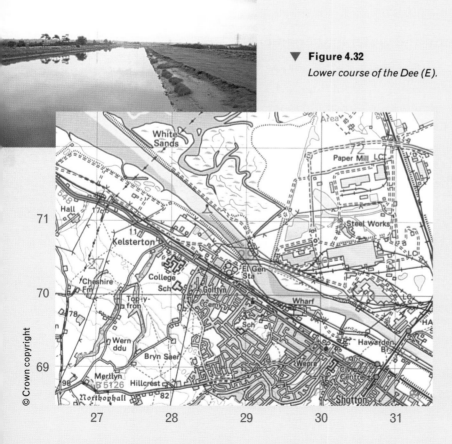

Figure 4.32
Lower course of the Dee (E).

© Crown copyright

Near Llangollen

The river valley then narrows to form a steep-sided gorge. The river's gradient becomes steeper as it flows over rapids at Llanollen (Figure 4.31). Layers of hard limestone on top of strong mudstones have resisted downcutting in this area. The steep valley sides show that little mass movement takes place on these strong rocks. At one time this important corridor of low land was defended by a castle (grid reference 223431). A main road from England follows the valley, and a canal and railway. Llangollen became an important local centre for trade as it took advantage of its situation. It is linear (long and thin) in shape, because the steep slopes have prevented it from expanding away from the river.

The lower course

Rivers are often used as boundaries, and the Dee forms the boundary between England and Wales for more than 15 km in its lower valley. The river is now in its lower course. Its large, slow-moving meanders do not extend over the full width of its floodplain, and there are some loops where the boundary is now on dry land close to the river. There is also evidence of abandoned meanders, where at first there would have been ox-bow lakes.

Approaching base level

As it nears the sea, the Dee becomes tidal. The channel has been straightened from its original course (Figure 4.32). It used to meander across a wide, marshy floodplain. Nearby Chester grew up on the lowest dry bridge point inland from the river mouth. The river has been straightened to allow water to flow to the sea more quickly and therefore prevent flooding. Flooding is a serious hazard, as the Dee's mountain headwaters often receive heavy rain. The surrounding flat land is protected by 5-metre high banks which have been built on either side of the river. The marshland areas have been drained, and now provide space for industry. There was a large steelworks at Shotton (now closed) which took advantage of the cheap land and plentiful water supply.

Unit 4 Landforms, Landscapes and Physical Processes

Activities

1 Examine **Figures 4.28–4.32**. Make a list of all the landforms found in the Dee valley which are a result of:

  a river erosion

  b river deposition.

2 Using labelled diagrams, explain how four of these landforms have been created. Choose two erosional and two depositional features.

3 Explain how a river's ability to erode and deposit is affected by:

  a river gradient

  b the volume of water (discharge) in the river

  c the strength and particle size of the surrounding soil and rock.

4 Complete a table like the one below to show how the river Dee and the valley landforms it has created have affected people at the five locations A–E on **Figure 4.28**.

Location	Advantages	Disadvantages
A	Protected from strong winds	Too steep for buildings – only suitable for sheep farming

5 **a** Describe how the river and its floodplain have been changed by people at location E.

  b Why have people made these changes?

  c Can you identify disadvantages resulting from such changes?

River systems and water management

A river can be thought of as a component of the **hydrosphere**, the system containing all the water on Earth (Figure 4.33). Like an ecosystem (see Unit 3), the hydrosphere consists of **flows** and **stores** (Figure 4.34). Rivers may not hold much of the Earth's water, but they are very important to people.

The area that a river collects its water from is called a **drainage basin**. The boundary of the drainage basin is the **watershed** (see Figure 4.37).

▼ **Figure 4.33**

The hydrological cycle as a system.

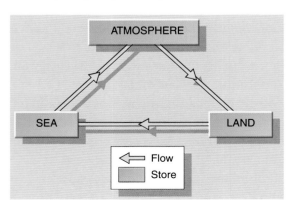

▶ **Figure 4.34**

Stored water in the hydrosphere.

Store	% of the world's water
Oceans	93.93
Underground water	4.12
Ice	1.65
Transfer between stores	0.27
Rivers and lakes	0.0289
Soil	0.001
Atmosphere	0.0001

Any rain that falls within the drainage basin begins a journey towards the sea. It may never get there. The time it takes for the water to reach the sea depends on several factors relating to the stores and flows of the basin:

Flows/Outputs	Stores
Evapotranspiration	Interception by vegetation
Surface run-off (overland flow)	Surface storage
Throughflow	Soil moisture
Percolation	Groundwater
Groundwater flow	

Activity

On a copy of **Figure 4.35**, add the appropriate labels from the table above.

▼ **Figure 4.35**
The drainage basin system.

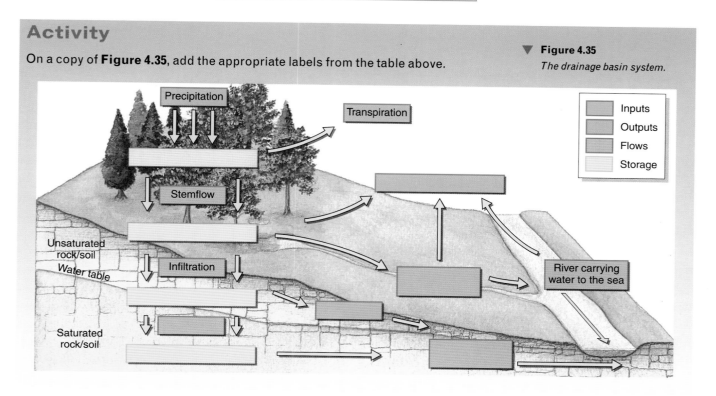

To compare drainage basins we can use measurements of the river discharge. This is measured in cumecs – that is, cubic metres (of water) per second. The balance between the stores and flows within a drainage basin, which influences discharge, depends on a number of factors:

- **Angle of slope** The steeper the slope of the valley, the faster the water enters the river.

- **Drainage density** The more tributaries the river has, the more water enters the river.

- **Geology** Impermeable rocks mean that more water flows overland.

- **Climate** The amount of rain and the temperature affect the amount of water entering the system and being lost to evaporation.

- **Land use** Forests intercept more rainfall than grass does. Urban areas and bare soil do not intercept much rainfall at all.

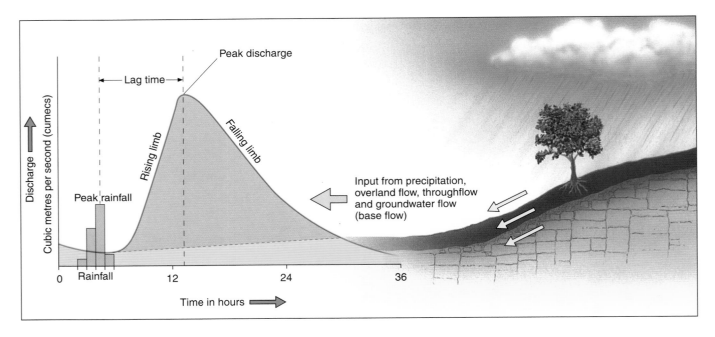

▲ **Figure 4.36**
A storm hydrograph.

▼ **Figure 4.37**
The basin of the river Torridge in north-west Devon.

Activities

Look carefully at **Figure 4.36**.

1 **a** How long after the rainfall peak was the peak discharge?

   b What is this period of time called?

2 **a** For how many hours was the storm run-off increasing?

   b What is this period called?

3 **a** For how many hours was the storm run-off decreasing?

   b What is this period called?

The drainage basin of the river Torridge: a case study

The river Torridge is in north-west Devon (Figure 4.37). The main river flows for 76.7 km from its source to the sea at Bideford. It has a number of tributaries, including the Lew, Okement and Waldon.

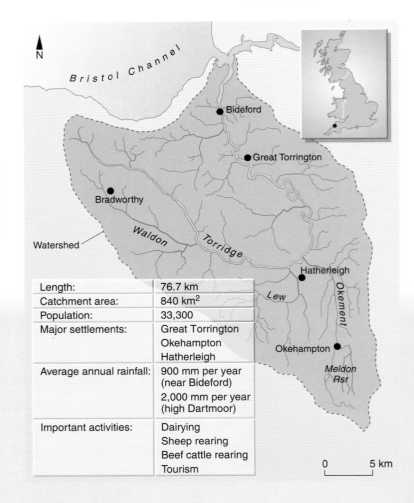

Length:	76.7 km
Catchment area:	840 km^2
Population:	33,300
Major settlements:	Great Torrington Okehampton Hatherleigh
Average annual rainfall:	900 mm per year (near Bideford) 2,000 mm per year (high Dartmoor)
Important activities:	Dairying Sheep rearing Beef cattle rearing Tourism

Unit 4 **Landforms, Landscapes and Physical Processes**

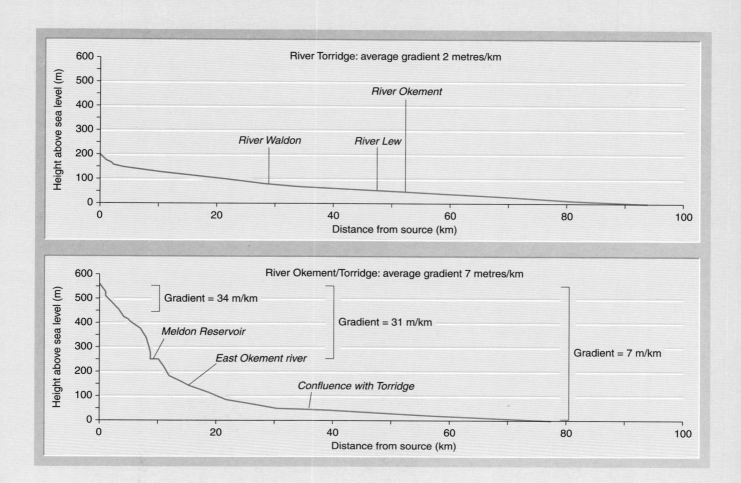

River Torridge: average gradient 2 metres/km

River Okement

River Waldon   *River Lew*

Height above sea level (m) / Distance from source (km)

River Okement/Torridge: average gradient 7 metres/km

Gradient = 34 m/km

Meldon Reservoir

Gradient = 31 m/km

East Okement river

Gradient = 7 m/km

Confluence with Torridge

Height above sea level (m) / Distance from source (km)

◀ **Figure 4.39**
▼ *Forestry plantations in the Torridge catchment area.*

▲ **Figure 4.38**
River profiles of the Torridge and the Okement.

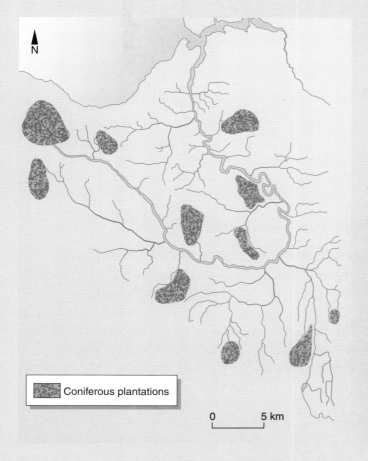

N

Coniferous plantations

0   5 km

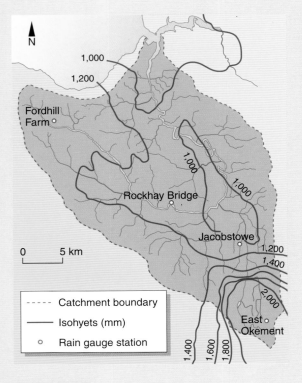

▲ Figure 4.40
Rainfall in the Torridge catchment area, December 1994.

Catchment boundary
Isohyets (mm)
Rain gauge station

Date	River Torridge		River Okement	
	Rainfall measured at Fordhill Form	Flow measured at Rockhay Bridge	Rainfall measured at East Okement	Flow measured at Jacobstowe
1	0.0	3.0	0.0	1.5
2	28.4	2.8	17.0	1.4
3	9.5	9.0	6.4	4.4
4	1.5	9.2	2.1	3.1
5	17.2	13.7	18.1	6.6
6	35.6	19.0	17.7	7.6
7	25.5	31.2	25.4	9.4
8	11.0	50.1	9.0	14.0
9	2.2	17.4	1.9	7.6
10	3.3	15.2	4.0	6.2
11	0.1	11.5	0.1	4.5
12	0.0	8.9	0.1	3.6
13	1.3	7.3	2.1	3.4
14	0.0	6.2	0.0	3.0

Activity

1 Use **Figures 4.37–4.40** to complete the following table.

Feature	Torridge	Okement
Angle of slope		
Drainage density		
Geology	Low permeability, little groundwater flow	Low permeability, little groundwater flow
Vegetation		
Rainfall		

2 a Now draw a storm hydrograph for each of the two rivers.

  b Write a description of the two hydrographs using the correct terms (see **Figure 4.36**).

3 Use the information you have collected in activity 1 to explain the differences between the two hydrographs.

Managing a river system

Like most rivers in the UK, the river Torridge now has a 'catchment management plan'. The National Rivers Authority (NRA) produced this plan. It sets out its aim like this:

'We will protect and improve the water environment by the effective management of water resources and by substantial reductions in pollution. We will aim to provide effective defence for people and property against flooding from rivers and the sea.'

In the plan the NRA identifies 19 different issues that it hopes to tackle by the year 1999. These include the following:

Activity

For each of the issues in the list on the right, say why you think the **NRA** considers it important to take action.

- Improving farm waste management.
- Monitoring the impact of coniferous plantations.
- Improving effluent control.
- Adopting a water resources strategy.
- Reversing the decline of salmon and trout stocks.
- Providing new flood defence works.

Managing the river Nile

The river Torridge is about 100 km long. The river Nile is 6,670 km long (it is the longest river in the world). Like the Torridge, the Nile is also 'managed', in order to provide for the people of Egypt. The Nile has been managed since the 1860s.

The drainage basin of the Nile covers an area of 3,000 square kilometres. The two main rivers feeding the Nile are the Blue Nile, which rises in the mountains of Ethiopia, and the White Nile, which flows through Sudan from the mountains and lakes of East Africa (Figure 4.41). In the past, the river used to flood each year. The flooding had several important effects. Each year the river transported 15 million tonnes of silt. It deposited most of this on its floodplain. Where it flows through the desert, the Nile has laid down a layer of sediment 10 metres thick, creating a fertile strip of land 15–20 km wide on either side of the river. The sediment also built up the mouth of the river, creating the Nile delta (Figure 4.42). These fertile areas form the basis of Egyptian agriculture – because of the river it is possible to grow crops all year round.

▼ **Figure 4.41**

  a *The course of the river Nile.*

  b *Annual flows of the Blue and White Niles at Khartoum, where they meet.*

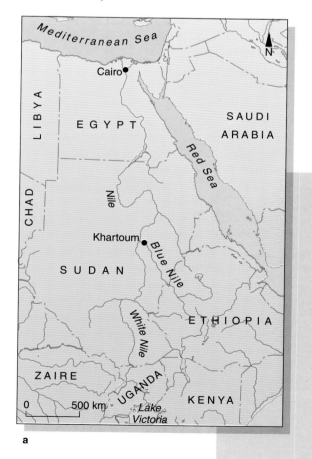

a

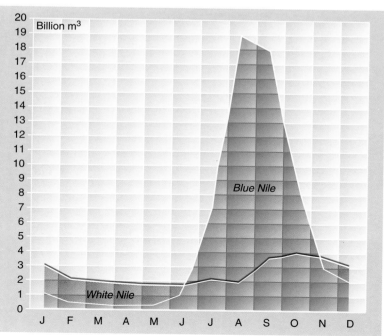

b

Sheep grazing in the Nile delta

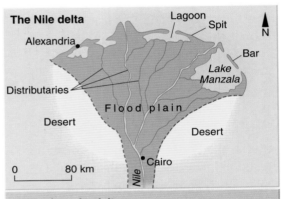

The Nile delta

Lagoon
Spit
Alexandria
Bar
Lake Manzala
Distributaries
Flood plain
Desert
Desert
Cairo
Nile
0   80 km

Formation of a delta
Stage 1
Deposition divides the river mouth into several distributaries. *Spits*, *bars* and *lagoons* form. The river extends into the sea via distributaries.

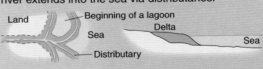

Land
Beginning of a lagoon
Sea
Delta
Sea
Distributary

Stage 2
Sediment begins to fill the lagoons, and they become swampy.

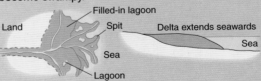

Filled-in lagoon
Land
Spit
Delta extends seawards
Sea
Sea
Lagoon

Stage 3
The older part of the delta is colonised by plants, and its height is slowly raised. Swamps gradually disappear and this part of the delta becomes dry land.

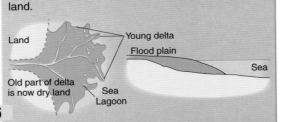

Land
Young delta
Flood plain
Sea
Old part of delta is now dry land
Sea
Lagoon

In 1861 a barrage was built across the Nile at the southern end of the delta, to control the water level and to provide water for irrigation and shipping in the delta. Since then eight more barrages and dams have been built across the Nile at various points. The biggest and most important is the Aswan High Dam, which was completed in 1970, and which created a huge lake, Lake Nasser. The dam was built:

- to control the flow of the river, thus reducing the flood danger to towns and villages

- to provide a water store for irrigation

- to produce electricity from a hydro-electric power station at the dam

- to create a new fishing industry in Lake Nasser.

However, the building of the dam created problems.

- A whole town had to be flooded when the lake was created.

- Less silt now flows down the river, so increasing amounts of fertiliser are needed by farmers along the Nile.

- Less silt also means that sea water now damages the soil in the delta, because it is not protected by the continually renewed layer of silt.

- Fish stocks in the delta have also declined because there is less food in the water.

- The annual flood also used to sweep away snails that carried the bilharzia organism which causes disease in humans.

Activities

1 Draw a map to show the course of the river Nile. In a box beside your map, add some important statistics about the river.

2 Explain how the Nile delta was formed. Now, speculate what may happen to it in the future.

3 a List (i) the benefits and (ii) the problems of building the Aswan dam.

  b Which people do you think (i) most benefited and (ii) least benefited from the building of the dam?

Weather and climate

Weather changes from day to day. Meteorologists – the people who study the weather – use records of the changing daily conditions of the atmosphere. From these they build up patterns of weather for a whole year. By calculating averages they establish 'average weather' in an area or region, and we call this climate.

When they study the weather, meteorologists rely on data collected every day from weather stations, for:

- maximum daily temperature

- minimum daily temperature

- air pressure

- rainfall
  ('precipitation' – rain, snow, hail, dew, frost)

- humidity

- wind speed and direction

- sunshine hours.

Daily weather recording sheet

Location:.....Northolt School...... Month..January 1997......

Observations made at 0900 GMT

Date	Maximum temperature (°C)	Minimum temperature (°C)	Rainfall (mm)
1	6.4	2.6	1.5
2	9.9	0.4	0.0
3	5.5	2.4	0.0
4	8.5	2.1	0.0
5	10.2	3.1	0.5
6	12.0	6.6	12.2

Increasingly, computers are used to collect these weather statistics. Many schools already have automatic computer weather recorders which allow them to monitor the weather on the school site. Once statistics have been collected, they can be used to look for patterns in the weather.

Activities

1 What is the difference between *weather* and *climate*?

2 Examine **Figure 4.43**. Try to match up the statistics required by the meteorologist with the instruments you can see in the photograph.

3 a Following the weather. Using either a regular TV weather forecast or a newspaper weather report, compile a record of weather variation for two contrasting locations in Britain, for example north-west Scotland and south-east England. Complete a table for a period of at least one week, like the one in **Figure 4.43**. You could add columns, for example for windspeed and direction, air, pressure, etc.

  b Examine the differences. Identify possible hypotheses which may explain the differences between the two locations. (*Hints:* Look for any links between the columns of data. What effects do altitude, latitude and distance from the sea have on the two places?)

▲ **Figure 4.43**
A weather station, and a typical weather recording sheet.

Climate patterns in Europe

Climates with similar characteristics can be grouped together. Figure 4.44 shows that Europe is made up of a jigsaw of different climate zones.

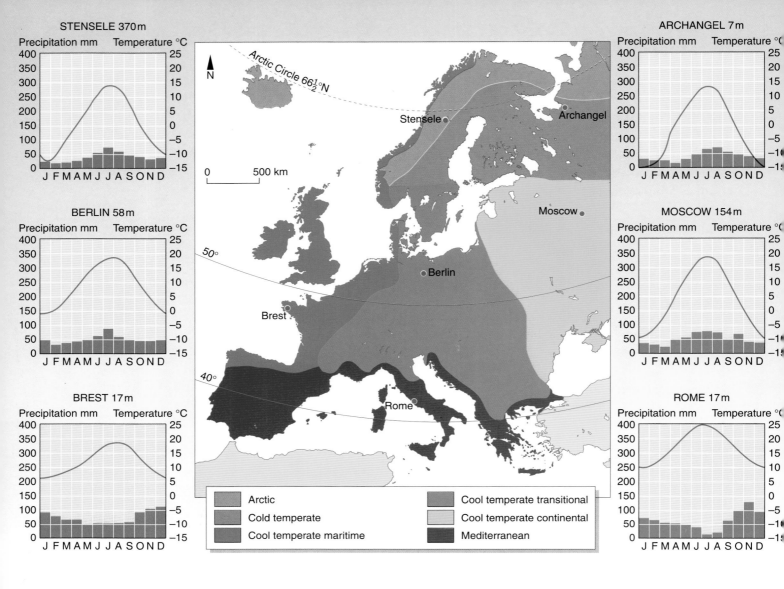

STENSELE 370m

Precipitation mm · Temperature °C

BERLIN 58m

Precipitation mm · Temperature °C

BREST 17m

Precipitation mm · Temperature °C

ARCHANGEL 7m

Precipitation mm · Temperature °C

MOSCOW 154m

Precipitation mm · Temperature °C

ROME 17m

Precipitation mm · Temperature °C

Arctic Circle 66½°N

Stensele · Archangel · Moscow · Berlin · Brest · Rome

50°

40°

0 — 500 km

Arctic	Cool temperate transitional
Cold temperate	Cool temperate continental
Cool temperate maritime	Mediterranean

▲ **Figure 4.44**

Europe's climatic zones.

Activities

1 Which are the main climate zones across Europe?

2 Describe the main features of each of these climate zones. For each one find out the average January temperature, the average July temperature, the total annual rainfall, and when most of the rain falls.

3 Collect evidence for and against each of the following hypotheses:
- Temperature and rainfall decrease from east to west.
- Temperature and rainfall decrease from north to south.

4 a Describe the effect of each of the following on the distribution of climate zones in Europe:
- latitude
- altitude
- distance from the Atlantic Ocean.

b Explain how each of these factors has an effect.

Extension activity

5 On-line computer information services such as CompuServe can provide weather information such as satellite images, statistics from weather stations, and weather maps (**Figure 4.45**). Use the service to produce a display of the weather for one continent over a 24-hour period.

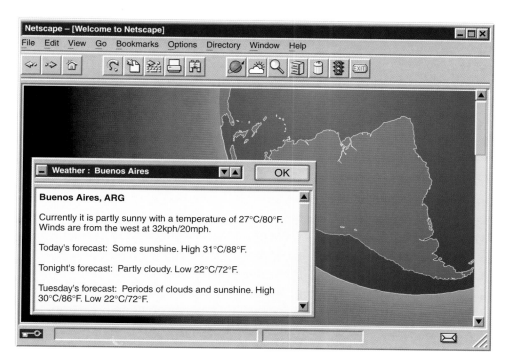

◀ Figure 4.45
Computer information on the weather.

Weather patterns in Europe

Day-to-day weather patterns in Europe can be far more extreme than the seasonal climatic patterns indicate.

The variability in European weather has a lot to do with the type of air mass affecting the continent. An air mass is a large area of air which has remarkably similar horizontal temperature and humidity. The air takes on the characteristics of its source region (remember, it is the ground that heats the air, not the sun directly). For example, air standing over the Arctic becomes cold and dry, whereas air over the Azores is warm and moist (Figure 4.47). Weather forecasters know what the air masses are like in their source regions. They are also able to predict how air will change as it moves away from its source. For example, as polar air from the Arctic moves over warmer seas, its lower layers become warmer and wetter.

▲ Figure 4.46
Newspaper headlines on the weather.

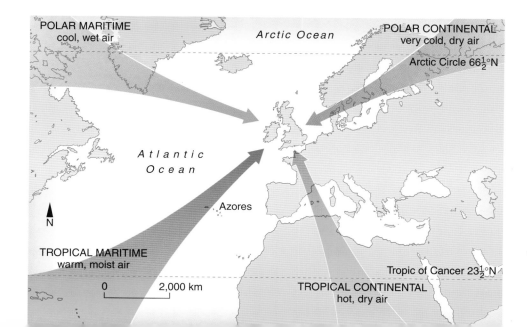

◀ Figure 4.47
Air masses affecting Europe.

Air masses are constantly moving. Air circulates from areas of high pressure to areas of low pressure, and because pressure changes frequently over north-western Europe, the airstream also varies a lot. This causes the weather to be very changeable. When a 'low' or depression passes over north-west Europe, it 'sucks in' air, sometimes from the north, sometimes from the south. When moist air is sucked in and drawn upwards by the low, masses of clouds form and rain falls.

Low pressure

In Britain we call low-pressure systems 'depressions'. Figure 4.48 shows a satellite image of a depression approaching north-west Europe, and a weather map of a depression over Scandinavia. As you can see, the depression is a huge spiral of cloud. It is formed as warm and cold air mix. Warm air rises over the colder air to form a warm front. Heavier, cold air moves underneath the warm air to form a cold front. As the depression passes overhead from west to east, a particular sequence of weather can be predicted: the fronts pass over and the winds change direction, bringing in air from different source regions.

Frontal rainfall is not the only type of rain we experience. See Figure 4.49.

High pressure

High-pressure systems or anticyclones bring settled weather, often with cloudless skies, both in winter and summer. In winter the Earth's heat can escape easily and this leads to frosty nights and very low temperatures. The days are often foggy because the cold ground causes water vapour in the air to condense. In summer high pressure brings hot, sunny, dry weather, although nights can still be chilly.

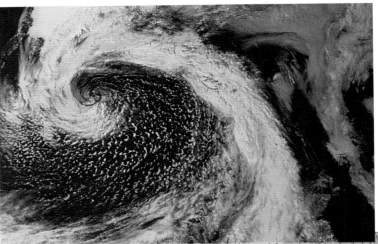

Figure 4.48

Satellite image and map of a depression over north-west Europe.

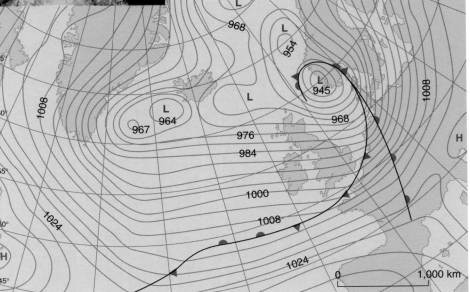

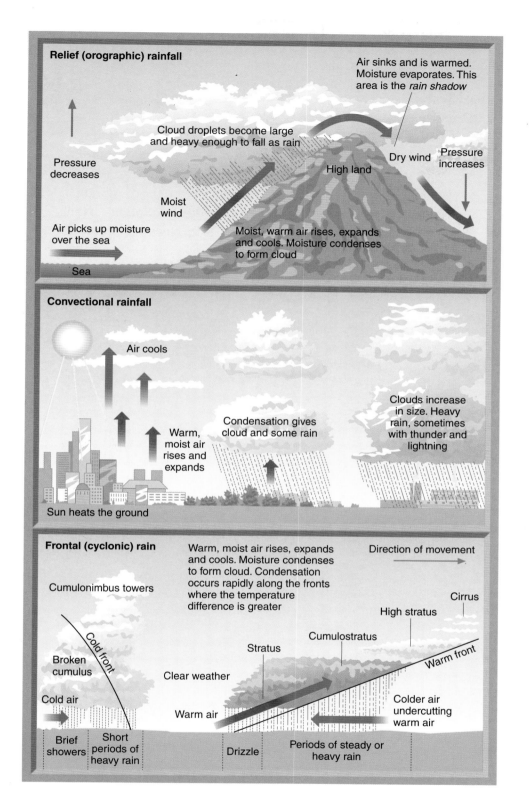

Figure 4.49

Frontal rainfall, relief rainfall and convectional rainfall.

Relief (orographic) rainfall

Air sinks and is warmed. Moisture evaporates. This area is the *rain shadow*

Cloud droplets become large and heavy enough to fall as rain

Pressure decreases

Dry wind

Pressure increases

High land

Moist wind

Air picks up moisture over the sea

Moist, warm air rises, expands and cools. Moisture condenses to form cloud

Sea

Convectional rainfall

Air cools

Clouds increase in size. Heavy rain, sometimes with thunder and lightning

Condensation gives cloud and some rain

Warm, moist air rises and expands

Sun heats the ground

Frontal (cyclonic) rain

Warm, moist air rises, expands and cools. Moisture condenses to form cloud. Condensation occurs rapidly along the fronts where the temperature difference is greater

Direction of movement

Cumulonimbus towers

Cirrus

High stratus

Cumulostratus

Stratus

Cold front

Clear weather

Warm front

Broken cumulus

Colder air undercutting warm air

Cold air

Warm air

Brief showers

Short periods of heavy rain

Drizzle

Periods of steady or heavy rain

Activity

Imagine you are a weather forecaster or meteorologist. You have been invited to give a short talk to a local sports club on: 'The weather: a national obsession'. Write the text of your talk, in which you explain how and why the British weather is so changeable.

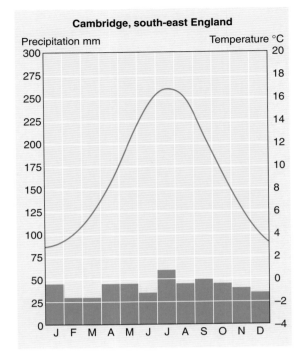

Cambridge, south-east England

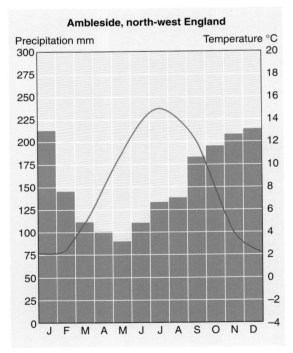

Ambleside, north-west England

▲ **Figure 4.50**

Climate graphs for Cambridge and Ambleside.

Climate and people

Even with all the new technology which gives us air conditioning and other ways of protecting ourselves from the climate, our lives are to some extent shaped by it. We can see this particularly in farming.

To show the difference climate can make to people's lives we look here at two farmers in the UK. One is in Suffolk, in south-east England, and the other is in the Cumbrian hills of north-west England. By reading the descriptions of their farms you should be able to pick up clues about how climate affects their lives.

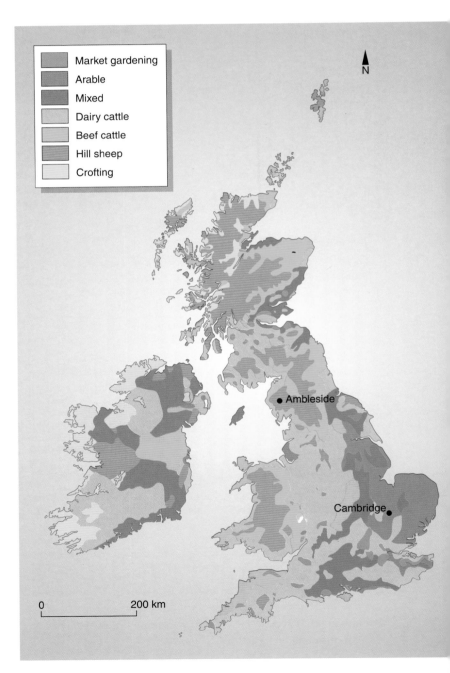

▶ **Figure 4.51**

Generalised map of agricultural land use in Britain.

John's farm in Suffolk

'My farm covers 1,620 hectares. It is an arable farm – my main crops are wheat, barley and sugarbeet, which are suited to the climate in the south-east. Wheat needs less than 750 mm of rain to grow well, and sugarbeet grows well with less than 650 mm a year and where summer temperatures rise above 15°C. The growing season is quite long here, with nine months of the year having an average temperature above 6°C (the minimum needed for plants to grow). With an average of 6.5–7 hours' sunshine a day in July and August, my crops ripen well. I do sometimes have crops flattened by heavy thunderstorms in the summer months. These can cause soil erosion on fields that have already been harvested.

The soil is fertile, made up of mainly thick loam and clay. It is broken up by hard frosts in winter, which makes it easier to plough. My land is fairly flat, and its average height is 52 metres above sea level. I'm fortunate to be able to keep 30,000 turkeys. These are supplied to supermarkets in London, 80 miles away.'

▲ **Figure 4.52**
View of John's farm in Suffolk.

▼ **Figure 4.53**
View of Judith's farm in Cumbria.

Judith's farm in the Cumbrian hills

'I keep a flock of 280 sheep on 134 hectares of land. Little else but sheep can withstand the harsh climate up here. Our land is between 228 and 304 metres above sea level. On the "fell" or hill tops, temperatures can be 3°C lower than they are down in the valley because they're exposed to strong winds. The annual rainfall exceeds 1,800 mm and temperatures are low in the summer, with an average of 5.5 hours of sunshine daily in July and August. Winters are cold, and we can be cut off by snow for days. On average only 5–6 months of the year have an average temperature above 6°C. We have to be careful at lambing time not to graze sheep on the slopes with a northerly aspect. Out of the sun, newly-born lambs are vulnerable to the cold. We grow some of our own hay as a fodder crop. This is important to feed the sheep in winter. Fodder is grown lower down where the soil is more fertile. The hay is harvested in July when it's dry. Our working days are very long at this time of year as we race to beat the rain.

Most of the soils on the farm are thin and acidic, and the high rainfall and low temperatures encourage peat formation. Waterlogged conditions on the soil surface prevent dead plant material from decomposing properly, and peat builds up.

The physical conditions on the farm limit what we can produce. Farming up here is a struggle – we barely make a living.'

Activities

1 Use the information in this section to complete a copy of this table:

	Annual rainfall	Annual average temperature	Altitude	Size of farm	Products
John's farm					
Judith's farm					

2 Use your table to help explain how the weather and climate affect **a** the ways that John and Judith run their farms, and **b** what is produced on each farm.

3 What other economic activities are shaped by the climate? In what ways does the climate have an effect?

The weather as a hazard

Extreme weather events can have a powerful effect on people. Each year a small number of people in Europe are killed by floods, lightning, wind, and heat waves. In tropical regions extreme weather conditions can be even more dangerous, because there they have more energy.

Figure 4.54
From The Observer,
22 October 1995.

DIARY OF THE PLANET

Flash floods

Heavy rains in the Indian coastal state of Andhra Pradesh killed 34 people and caused flash floods. Nearly 2,500 homes were damaged during downpours that began nine days ago.

Rainstorms in the southern China region of

Guangxi have left at least 46 people dead and 30,000 stranded, and washed away 10,000 head of livestock. The inundations were caused by tropical storm Ted moving ashore from the Gulf of Tonkin.

Tropical storms

Tropical storm Roxanne

rambled through the Gulf of Mexico, swamping Campeche and other coastal areas of the Mexican mainland as well as some offshore islands.

The worst devastation was on Isla del Carmen, a coastal shrimp-fishing island where surging tides swept away

thousands of tin and wood shacks.

Typhoon Ward formed over the Philippine Sea, then veered north-eastwards before reaching Japan. A weak and unnamed tropical cyclone formed briefly in the Arabian Sea, then lost force off the coast of Oman.

For example, hurricanes are similar to the depressions experienced in the UK (they are areas of low pressure), but they are much more intense. As the air pressure at the surface drops, winds begin to spiral inwards and upwards. This spiral is fed by warm, moist air which rises to form vast clouds. The clouds give heavy rain, and the winds can blow at over 150 km per hour. The storms can measure hundreds of kilometres across, and their paths are unpredictable.

Figure 4.55
The structure of a hurricane.

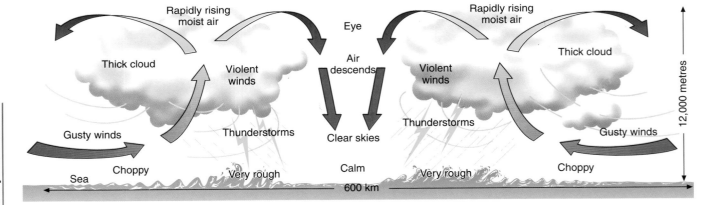

Activities

1 According to the newspaper article in **Figure 4.54**, which five areas were affected by tropical storms? Use an atlas map to find each of these places.

2 Using **Figure 4.55** to help you, describe the sequence of events if a hurricane were to pass directly overhead.

3 Tropical storms have tremendous power, but can you give other reasons why you think they cause so much damage?

Human influences on the weather and climate

Throughout the 1990s, argument has raged as to whether the Earth is experiencing global warming. This warming is blamed on the build-up of some gases, for example carbon dioxide, in the atmosphere. These gases contribute to the Earth's 'greenhouse effect' – on which all life depends – and their build-up may be making it stronger. Figure 4.56 outlines the main issues involved in global warming.

Many experts agree that global warming is happening. What no-one knows is exactly how it will affect the climates of the world (Figure 5.47). This is a story that will unfold during the rest of your life.

Activities

1 Which two sources of evidence are presented in the newspaper article to suggest that global warming has occurred?

2 What has happened to sea levels since 1900?

3 According to the records, how have air and surface temperatures changed since 1860?

▶ **Figure 4.56**
From The Guardian, *25 March 1995.*

Bird-watching helps clinch warming theory

Paul Brown on how scientists proved climatic change is really happening

AS COUNTRIES squabble over tackling greenhouse gas emissions, doubts about whether the earth is really getting warmer are being resolved with the help of bird-watchers and supercomputers at the Hadley Centre for Climatic Change in Berkshire.

Yesterday the British Trust for Ornithology put out results of years of watching tens of thousands of nests. 'Careful analysis shows how many common species are, on average, nesting earlier and producing bigger clutches of eggs and larger broods of nestlings,' it said.

While global warming may be good for birds, it is bad news for humans. Large areas of the world get far less rain under the computer predictions. The droughts in Southern Africa in the last 10 years fit almost exactly with predictions. What is significant about the new findings by the supercomputer at the Hadley Centre is that some of the data now match what is happening in Europe and North America.

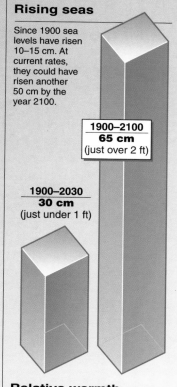

Rising seas

Since 1900 sea levels have risen 10–15 cm. At current rates, they could have risen another 50 cm by the year 2100.

1900–2100
65 cm
(just over 2 ft)

1900–2030
30 cm
(just under 1 ft)

Relative warmth

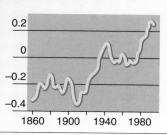

Land, air and sea surface temperature Index: 1951 to 1980 average = 0°C

▼ **Figure 4.57**
Principal world climate types.

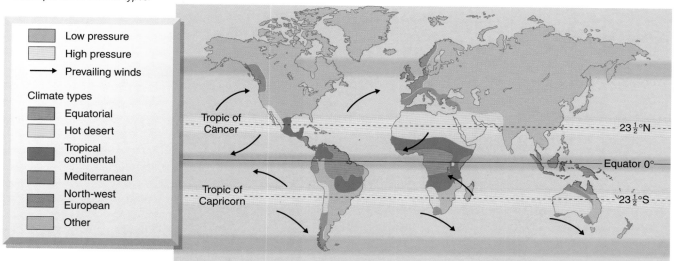

- Low pressure
- High pressure
- → Prevailing winds

Climate types
- Equatorial
- Hot desert
- Tropical continental
- Mediterranean
- North-west European
- Other

Tropic of Cancer

Tropic of Capricorn

23½°N

Equator 0°

23½°S

THINKING GEOGRAPHY

Globalisation

Think about the following events. All of them happened in 1997.

1 *The Ford motor company (which has its headquarters in Detroit, USA) announced that the Escort would no longer be made at Halewood near Liverpool: 1,500 people would lose their jobs. The new Escort would be made in Germany and Spain, and imported into Britain.*

2 *Thousands of workers went on strike in Seoul, South Korea, costing several billion pounds' worth of lost production from electronics factories and car factories. The South Korean government used the police to try to end the strike, but refused to remove its cause: a new law to reduce job security (ending the South Korean tradition that 'a job is for life'). This would make it easier for firms to sack workers.*

3 *The German government tried to reduce employment benefit available to people who lose their jobs, and to reduce the subsidy which pays for workers to visit a health spa. The government apparently wanted to end the reputation that German workers are the most pampered (and expensive) in the world.*

4 *Economists in Cambridge, UK, announced that the city and surrounding towns are set for such growth in the communications, electronics and biotechnology industries that it will dwarf the original 'Cambridge phenomenon'. The location of Cambridge, and its transport links, plus the 'world-class educational facilities', are given as the reasons for this. As many as 20,000 new high-tech jobs are expected in the region over the next few years.*

5 *When booking a flight on British Airways, in a London travel agent, a customer found that the ticket was produced – almost instantly – by computer operators in New Delhi, India.*

What these events have in common is that they are all part of a process which we now know as 'globalisation'.

What is globalisation?

An article in *The Guardian* described globalisation as the trend 'towards jobs, money, goods, information and people being transferred around the globe almost without restriction'. Globalisation is understood by many experts to be the inevitable result of technological progress: surely it is just the same as cars replacing horses, and steam power replacing sailing ships? But its effects are interesting and important to analyse.

The effects of globalisation

1 Some firms are perfect examples of the globalisation process. Take Ford, for example: the reasons for the company's decision to end production at Halewood were said to be part of their **global policy**. Ford has decided that it must make and sell **global cars** instead of different cars for different countries. This, they think, will be more efficient because it means they can rationalise and make larger numbers of cars in fewer factories. The trade unions at Halewood argued that the reason the British were the ones to lose out is that in Britain it is cheaper to make people redundant than, say, in Germany or Spain (the other places where Ford Escorts could be made). There, workers are more expensive, and redundancy payments would be higher.

2 On the other hand, some experts argue the opposite: globalised car manufacture means that Britain has attracted large numbers of factories (Honda and Nissan, for example) because its workforce is cheaper than that of other European countries.

3 Some experts have described globalisation as the 'Macdonaldisation' of our lives: all around the world it is in the interests of large, transnational companies to produce their goods and services to a predictable fixed standard, cheaply and efficiently. A hamburger bought from an international chain of restaurants is pretty much the same in Moscow, San Francisco, Tokyo or São Paulo – they are cheap, of reliable quality, and sell in enormous quantities. Although this makes huge profits for the restaurant chain, it can have negative effects:

- It reduces choice and diversity, because smaller restaurants cannot compete.

- It forces people to accept the standard. Henry Ford, the founder of the Ford motor company, is supposed to have said: 'You can have any color you want, so long as it is black.' These days cars are standardised in ways other than colour.

- It may encourage a kind of imperialism – the world dominated by a few very powerful suppliers of food, goods and services (e.g. Coca-Cola, Sony, American Express).

4 Globalisation has reduced the power of governments. In the USA and many European countries, the difference between the main political parties is small; they all believe in similar economic policies. This is because political parties feel they cannot resist the power of global markets. For example, if a few of the leading banks decided at the same time to move money out of London – and they can do this in seconds using computers – the entire finance industry could be sent into a spin and billions of pounds would 'disappear'. Governments have to be careful what they do and say.

Activities

You need to discuss the ideas on these pages to make sure you understand them. Then:

1 Make a list of further examples of globalisation. National newspapers are a good source of examples.

2 For each of the examples on page 126, write a couple of sentences to explain how it links with the idea of globalisation.

3 Analyse each example (or those you have found). What are the effects of the events on people in different parts of the world – their wealth, security and well-being?

Economic Activity and the Geography of Development

FOCUS

This unit investigates questions and issues about the geography of employment and economic development. The main ideas are summarised by the following focus statements:

- Employment structures vary at local, regional, national and global scales, and from place to place.
- Economic and social well-being can be measured in a variety of ways.
- Patterns of economic and social well-being can be identified at different scales, and vary from place to place.
- International trade is closely linked to economic development.
- Economic activity – for example the tourism industry – can seriously affect the physical environment.

- Leisure activities occur in a variety of physical and human environments.
- The impact of people's activities, such as leisure, on processes and landforms requires careful management.
- The recreation industry is now the world's biggest industry and is global in its extent and impact.

This unit is mainly about employment, and to help us investigate this we use examples from Europe (particularly Germany and the UK), the Pacific Rim (especially China) and South Africa.

Analysing employment structure

We can divide industry into three or four groups. Industries that extract or take things from the environment are called **primary industries**. These include farming, fishing, forestry and mining.

Secondary industries take the products of primary industry and make or manufacture things from them. All factories are within the secondary group.

Finally there are **tertiary** or **service industries**. These industries do not make anything, but instead sell goods or services. A good way to remember this is:

Primary: *taking*
Secondary: *making*
Tertiary: *selling* or *helping*.

In recent years a growing part of the tertiary group has been identified by experts as a new **quaternary** group. This consists of research and development industries, and people employed in the 'knowledge' industries. Thus we can add the fourth group:

Quaternary: *thinking and experimenting*.

In the UK the government collects statistics on industry using what is called the **Standard Industrial Classification**, or SIC (Figure 5.1). This divides industry into categories, although it is still possible to divide these into the main groups listed on page 128.

▼ **Figure 5.1**
Standard Industrial Classification.

SIC code	Industry	1981			1994		
		Males (%)	Females (%)	Total workforce (thousands)	Males (%)	Females (%)	Total workforce (thousands)
0	Agriculture, forestry, fishing	2.2	1.0	360.7	1.8	0.6	260.3
1	Energy & water supply	4.9	1.0	708.8	2.2	0.7	314.6
2	Metals, minerals & chemicals	5.9	2.1	937.1	4.0	1.4	585.5
3	Metal goods, engineering & vehicle industries	18.4	6.5	2,917.9	13.4	3.6	1,845.5
4	Other manufacturing	10.9	10.6	2,358.3	10.3	7.2	1,890.7
5	Construction	8.1	1.2	1,129.5	6.8	1.3	880.4
6	Distribution, hotels & catering, repairs	15.2	24.3	4,176.8	19.5	23.9	4,662.3
7	Transport & communications	9.1	3.0	1,423.1	8.5	2.8	1,225.7
8	Banking, finance, insurance, business services & leasing	7.2	9.0	1,744.2	12.3	12.8	2,705.4
9	Public administration & other services	18.1	41.3	6,127.4	21.2	45.7	7,169.7
	Total workers			21,883.8			21,540.1

One of the problems of using statistics is that the people who compile them often change the way in which they present them. For instance, the UK government introduced a new SIC in 1996. This means that it will be harder to compare statistics before and after 1996. The new SIC categories are as follows:

0 Agriculture, forestry, fishing, hunting

1 Mining, quarrying

2 Manufacturing

3 Electricity, gas, water

4 Distribution, hotels & catering, repairs

5 Construction

6 Transport, storage, communications

7 Financial & business services

8 Public administration & defence

9 Education, social work, health services

10 Other

The proportion of people employed in different industrial groups makes up the industrial structure of an area. It is possible to look at industrial structure at regional, national and continental scales. The industrial structure of an area can give us an insight into the economic and social well-being of its population.

Figure 5.2 shows the way in which the industrial structure of the UK has changed between 1901 and 1991, and Figure 5.3 shows industrial structure for the standard UK regions. The newspaper articles in Figure 5.4 highlight five trends in employment.

▶ **Figure 5.2**
Industrial structure of the UK, 1901–1991.

Year	Primary (%)	Secondary (%)	Tertiary (%)	Working population (thousands)
1901	17.9	41.3	40.8	18,276
1911	17.5	39.7	42.8	20,171
1921	14.6	39.7	45.7	19,759
1931	11.8	38.4	49.8	20,932
1941	9.3	45.5	45.2	24,894
1951	9.2	44.7	46.1	23,810
1961	7.0	45.5	47.5	25,344
1971	3.6	46.5	49.9	23,446
1981	3.0	35.6	61.4	21,893
1991	1.7	27.1	71.2	22,234

▶ **Figure 5.3**
Industrial structure in the UK Standard Regions, 1994.

UK Standard Region	Agriculture (%)	Industry (%)	Services (%)	Total male working population (thousands)
North	1.7	29.3	68.2	1,263.1
Yorkshire & Humberside	1.7	30.8	66.9	2,176.7
East Midlands	2.9	34.7	62.0	1,852.8
East Anglia	4.4	28.9	66.3	993.6
South East	1.0	21.9	76.5	8,137.1
South West	3.3	26.0	70.2	2,179.0
West Midlands	1.9	35.7	61.6	2,338.9
North West	0.7	30.5	68.2	2,678.0
Wales	4.3	29.7	65.6	1,175.5
Scotland	3.4	27.5	68.5	2,261.4
Northern Ireland	5.3	24.1	69.5	600.5
UK total	2.1	27.6	69.7	25,656.7

▼ **Figure 5.4**
Recent trends in employment.

Jobs for the Girls

Imagine you've been transported from the 1950s into a 1990s' office. You'll be struck by the computers, by the fact that the paperless office hasn't arrived and by the absence of tapping typewriters. But more than anything you'll be surprised at what the women are doing.

A generation ago women's work and men's work were different. Men were managers, women were secretaries. Men did the hard industrial labour on building sites or in factories, women did the fiddly assembly jobs. Fewer than one woman in a hundred worked as a professional: most did all their work in the home.

Now the picture has changed. Women may still be a minority in the boardroom or Cabinet, but they make up almost half of the workforce. Nor are they just stuck in low-paid jobs. There are now more women solicitors under 30 than men, and more women professionals under 35 than over.

Evening Standard, 31 August 1995

Changing Patterns of Employment

The story here is shown in the graphs taken from the new Labour Force Survey. They chart the 10-year development of our job market. Three points stand out. One is that full-time employment for men is still well below the level of a decade ago. The second is that part-time employment both men and women has climbed steadily through both boom and slump. The third is that self-employment, though bumpy, has tended to climb for both men and women.

A further nugget of information, not shown in the graphs, but consistent with the rise both of part-time work and of self-employment, is that the number of people with multiple employment is also climbing at the moment. No less than 1,280,000 of us now have at least two jobs.

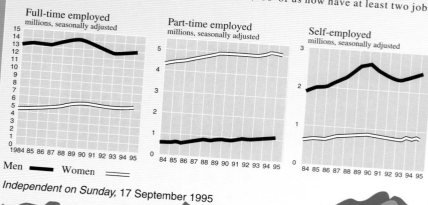

Independent on Sunday, 17 September 1995

Activities

1 a Devise a graph to show the changing industrial structure in the UK between 1901 and 1991.

  b Describe the trends shown by your graph.

2 Look at the possible reasons for change to industrial structure listed below.

  a On a copy of the following table, add the reasons to the correct columns (some may go in more than one column).

Declining primary employment	Declining secondary employment	Increasing tertiary employment

Possible reasons

- Increased efficiency of farms
- Introduction of machinery to replace workers
- Imports of cheaper products from abroad
- Introduction of public transport systems
- Creation of the National Health Service
- Development of compulsory schooling for all
- Loss of markets due to the end of the British Empire
- Exhaustion of raw materials

  b Try to add one more 'possible reason' of your own to each column of your table.

3 a On copies of **Figure 5.5**, produce three maps to show the regional distribution of primary, secondary and tertiary industries. You should use a five-colour key for your maps to show the following categories:

Less than 5%	41–60%
6–20%	More than 60%
21–40%	

  b For each sector suggest why particular regions have high or low figures. A good atlas will help you.

4 a Use the figures in **Figure 5.1** to devise a graph to show the changing employment pattern in each industrial category.

  b Identify the five trends in UK employment patterns highlighted by the items in **Figure 5.4**.

5 It is the year 2010. Imagine that you are a young person looking for a job. Write a letter to an elderly relative explaining the differences between employment in the year 2010 and in 1990. Think about all the trends you have seen in this section, and project them into the future.

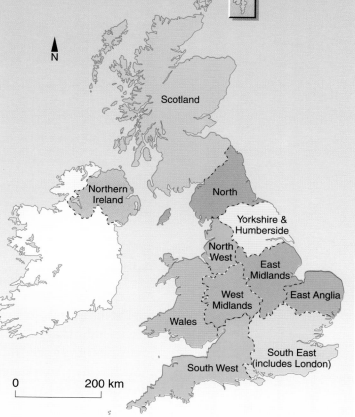

▼ **Figure 5.5**
The UK Standard Regions.

Industrial structure: the global pattern

Figure 5.6 presents information on the industrial structure of some of the countries already looked at in this book. It is possible to use industrial structure to give a picture of economic development within a country. The idea of development is a complicated one, but often it is 'measured' in terms of how wealthy a country is. The measure used is the **gross national product per capita**, or GNP. This is the value of all goods and services produced by a country, divided by its population. It gives an idea of how much each person in the country would receive if all the money earned was divided equally amongst them.

▶ **Figure 5.6**

The GNP of selected countries.

Country	GNP per capita (US$ 1991)	% primary	% secondary	% tertiary
Japan	26,920	3	42	55
Germany	23,650	2	39	59
Iceland	22,580	10	15	75
USA	22,560	2	29	69
Canada	21,260	3	21	76
France	20,600	3	29	68
UK	16,750	2	37	61
Brazil	2,920	10	39	51
Mexico	2,870	9	30	61
South Africa	2,600	5	44	51
Philippines	740	21	34	45
Egypt	630	18	30	52
China	370	27	42	31
India	330	31	27	42

Activities

1 Draw scattergraphs to show the relationship between:

  a GNP and primary industry

  b GNP and secondary industry

  c GNP and tertiary industry.

2 For each graph, write a sentence like this one to describe your results:

  'The higher the level of primary industry in a country, the lower the GNP per capita.'

Adding value

As you can see from your scattergraphs, countries that rely on primary products tend to have a low GNP, whilst those that have high levels of secondary and tertiary industries have a higher GNP. This is because secondary and tertiary industries have added more value to their products, so they are able to charge more for them. For example, when a tree is cut down it can be sold as timber. If the wood is treated and sawn into boards and planks it can be sold for more money. If the treated wood is made into a product such as a table or chair, it can be sold for even more money. **Value** has been added at each stage.

The wealthiest countries are those that can afford most services, particularly education, and research industries.

Development: is it all about money?

GNP per capita is not the only measure used to show what life in a country is like. Many people think this measure is unreliable because there are vast differences between the rich and poor in any country, and particularly in developing countries. The **average figure** therefore means very little. The United Nations uses a measure called the **Human Development Index** (Figure 5.7). This takes into account not only national income but also factors such as life expectancy and statistics for education in the country. The UN believes that development is about people's quality of life – that is, the way in which a country chooses to spend its money, and not just the **amount** that it creates.

▼ **Figure 5.7**
The Human Development Index for selected countries.

Country	Japan	Germany	Iceland	USA	Canada	France	UK	Brazil	Mexico	South Africa	Philippines	Egypt	China	India
HDI	0.981	0.955	0.958	0.976	0.982	0.969	0.962	0.739	0.804	0.674	0.600	0.385	0.610	0.297

Activities

1 Select an example of a primary product. Write a description to show the idea of 'adding value'.

2 a Which countries have a higher placing according to the Human Development Index (**Figure 5.7**) than according to the figures for GNP (**Figure 5.6**)?

  b In each case, suggest why this may be so.

3 From the following list, choose the three most important indicators that you would include as measures of 'quality of life'. Explain why you chose these indicators.

  • Adult literacy

  • Population per doctor

  • Access to clean water

  • Life expectancy

  • Income

  • Percentage of children attending secondary school

  • Number of universities

  • Crime rate

Primary industry on a continental scale: agriculture in the EU

A hundred and fifty years ago the majority of people in Europe were employed in a primary industry – agriculture. Farming was the principal industrial activity throughout the world. Today the numbers employed in agriculture are very different (Figure 5.8).

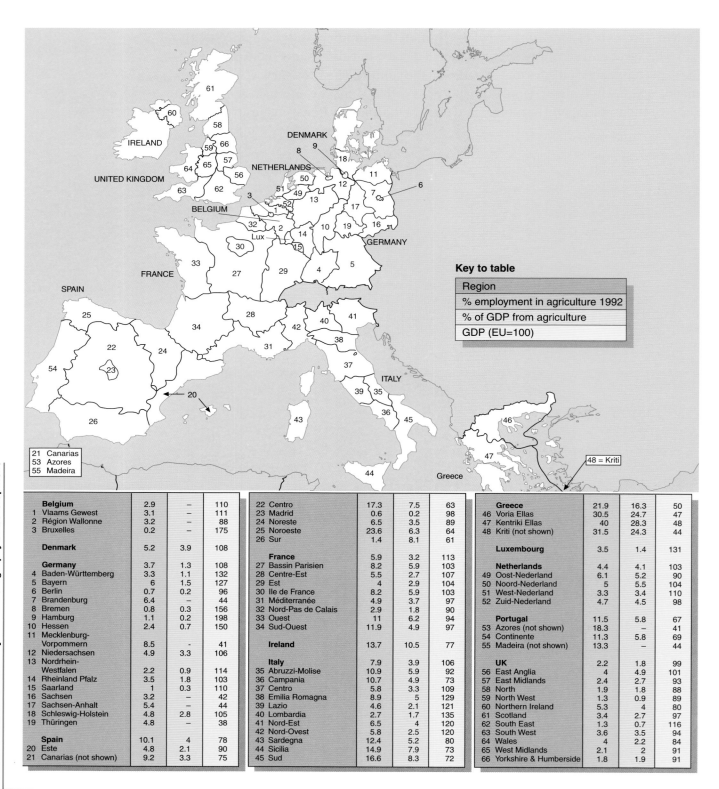

Key to table

Region
% employment in agriculture 1992
% of GDP from agriculture
GDP (EU=100)

21	Canarias
53	Azores
55	Madeira

Region	% emp.	% GDP	GDP
Belgium	2.9	–	110
1 Vlaams Gewest	3.1	–	111
2 Région Wallonne	3.2	–	88
3 Bruxelles	0.2	–	175
Denmark	5.2	3.9	108
Germany	3.7	1.3	108
4 Baden-Württemberg	3.3	1.1	132
5 Bayern	6	1.5	127
6 Berlin	0.7	0.2	96
7 Brandenburg	6.4	–	44
8 Bremen	0.8	0.3	156
9 Hamburg	1.1	0.2	198
10 Hessen	2.4	0.7	150
11 Mecklenburg-Vorpommern	8.5	-	41
12 Niedersachsen	4.9	3.3	106
13 Nordrhein-Westfalen	2.2	0.9	114
14 Rheinland Pfalz	3.5	1.8	103
15 Saarland	1	0.3	110
16 Sachsen	3.2	–	42
17 Sachsen-Anhalt	5.4	–	44
18 Schleswig-Holstein	4.8	2.8	105
19 Thüringen	4.8	–	38
Spain	10.1	4	78
20 Este	4.8	2.1	90
21 Canarias (not shown)	9.2	3.3	75

Region	% emp.	% GDP	GDP
22 Centro	17.3	7.5	63
23 Madrid	0.6	0.2	98
24 Noreste	6.5	3.5	89
25 Noroeste	23.6	6.3	64
26 Sur	1.4	8.1	61
France	5.9	3.2	113
27 Bassin Parisien	8.2	5.9	103
28 Centre-Est	5.5	2.7	107
29 Est	4	2.9	104
30 Ile de France	8.2	5.9	103
31 Méditerranée	4.9	3.7	97
32 Nord-Pas de Calais	2.9	1.8	90
33 Ouest	11	6.2	94
34 Sud-Ouest	11.9	4.9	97
Ireland	13.7	10.5	77
Italy	7.9	3.9	106
35 Abruzzi-Molise	10.9	5.9	92
36 Campania	10.7	4.9	73
37 Centro	5.8	3.3	109
38 Emilia Romagna	8.9	5	129
39 Lazio	4.6	2.1	121
40 Lombardia	2.7	1.7	135
41 Nord-Est	6.5	4	120
42 Nord-Ovest	5.8	2.5	120
43 Sardegna	12.4	5.2	80
44 Sicilia	14.9	7.9	73
45 Sud	16.6	8.3	72

Region	% emp.	% GDP	GDP
Greece	21.9	16.3	50
46 Voria Ellas	30.5	24.7	47
47 Kentriki Ellas	40	28.3	48
48 Kriti (not shown)	31.5	24.3	44
Luxembourg	3.5	1.4	131
Netherlands	4.4	4.1	103
49 Oost-Nederland	6.1	5.2	90
50 Noord-Nederland	5	5.5	104
51 West-Nederland	3.3	3.4	110
52 Zuid-Nederland	4.7	4.5	98
Portugal	11.5	5.8	67
53 Azores (not shown)	18.3	–	41
54 Continente	11.3	5.8	69
55 Madeira (not shown)	13.3	–	44
UK	2.2	1.8	99
56 East Anglia	4	4.9	101
57 East Midlands	2.4	2.7	93
58 North	1.9	1.8	88
59 North West	1.3	0.9	89
60 Northern Ireland	5.3	4	80
61 Scotland	3.4	2.7	97
62 South East	1.3	0.7	116
63 South West	3.6	3.5	94
64 Wales	4	2.2	84
65 West Midlands	2.1	2	91
66 Yorkshire & Humberside	1.8	1.9	91

As you can see, the importance of agriculture varies across the countries of the EU. As with world patterns, areas with high levels of agriculture generally have lower GDP figures. However, there are some exceptions such as the Paris Basin, Emilia Romagna, Noord-Nederland and East Anglia. In these areas farms are highly mechanised, operate on a large scale and are very profitable. In areas such as Greece, southern Italy and Portugal, on the other hand, farming is usually small scale and operates in difficult conditions (Figure 5.9).

Just because the percentage of workers employed in agriculture has declined, it does not mean that agriculture has declined in importance. In 1850 the population of all EU countries was about 150 million. Today it is close to 326 million. Therefore the amount of food needed to feed the population has doubled.

European farming has generally been a success. For example, when the Common Market (which was to become the EU) was set up in 1951, one of its top priorities was the creation of a stable agricultural system that met the needs of farmers and consumers. This goal was tackled through the Common Agricultural Policy, or CAP. Throughout the history of the EU the CAP has been controversial, partly because of the huge sums of money involved.

▼ **Figure 5.9**
Areas designated by the European Union as 'Mountainous' and 'Less favoured'.

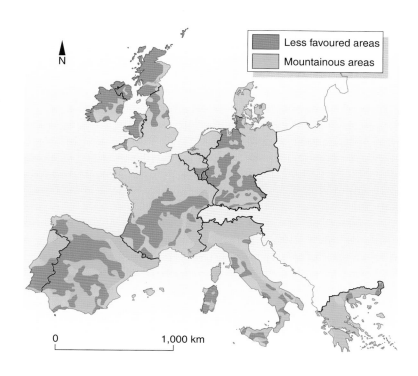

Less favoured areas

Mountainous areas

0   1,000 km

The CAP's main aims were:

• to make food available to European consumers at reasonable prices

• to make sure farmers had a fair return for their efforts.

The CAP takes over half of all the money spent by the EU (Figure 5.10).

Year	Consumer price index for foodstuffs	Price index for agricultural products	CAP as % of the EU budget
1985	100.0	100.0	70.2
1986	104.4	101.7	67.7
1987	107.3	101.5	–
1988	110.2	103.9	63.2
1989	116.5	113.1	60.2
1990	123.4	114.8	59.3
1991	130.4	117.9	58.1
1992	–	–	58.2

◀ **Figure 5.10**
The cost of agriculture in the EU.

CAP Changes

* Prices for cereals and beef cut radically.

* Part of the land used for cereals taken out of production as 'set-aside', a scheme that pays farmers not to grow any crops.

* Farmers who lost income compensated.

* Support given to environmentally friendly farmers.

* Early retirement schemes to create room for younger farmers.

* Support for changing land use, from farming to less managed sites and woodland.

* If production in the EU of a crop exceeds a set level, the price to the farmer is reduced (this measure discourages the production of surpluses).

* Limits placed on milk production (milk quotas).

▲ **Figure 5.11**
The 1992 CAP reforms.

▼ **Figure 5.12**
Change in agriculture in the EU.

One of the main reasons for the large sums of money involved in the CAP was production and price guarantees. Farmers were guaranteed a price for their crop, however much of that crop was produced. This encouraged farmers to become more efficient, and to increase the size of their farms. (In fact, 80 per cent of CAP spending went to only 20 per cent of farmers – the ones who ran large, well-organised farms. Small family farms did less well, and many farmers in poorer areas were forced to leave the land.) As a result there was a surplus of many products, some of which were sold at subsidised prices to the rest of the world. In 1992 the CAP was reformed in order to tackle this problem (Figure 5.11). Figure 5.12 shows the changing pattern of agriculture across the EU as a result of the CAP reforms.

Activities

1 What were the original aims of the CAP?

2 In your opinion, in what ways was the CAP successful and/or unsuccessful?

3 Use the statistics in **Figure 5.12** to show how employment in farming has changed in the countries of the EU since 1975.

4 a What measures were introduced in 1992 to reduce the *cost* of the CAP?

   b According to the statistics in **Figure 5.12**, in what ways do you think the 1992 reforms have worked?

5 What do you think are the advantages and disadvantages of 'set-aside'? You could organise your answer under two headings: 'Economic' and 'Environmental'.

Country	Total farmworkers		No. of farms		Self-sufficiency (%)					
					In wheat		In milk		In beef	
	1975	1990	1980	1987	1986	1993	1986	1993	1986	1993
Belgium	140,000	119,000	115,000	93,000	69	54	113	–	137	–
Denmark	177,000	147,000	123,000	87,000	105	113	101	101	282	198
Germany	1,234,000	1,081,000	850,000	705,000	98	117	72	106	121	108
Greece	–	889,000	–	953,000	104	114	96	99	32	31
France	1,950,000	1,394,000	1,255,000	982,000	–	249	98	104	117	116
Ireland	325,000	173,000	224,000	217,000	55	98	78	100	678	1,243
Italy	2,826,000	1,913,000	2,634,000	2,784,000	55	92	92	95	58	64
Luxembourg	12,000	6,000	5,000	4,000	77	54	113	101	137	178
Netherlands	254,000	289,000	149,000	132,000	47	29	325	89	219	–
Portugal	–	840,000	–	635,000	34	34	70	99	86	68
Spain	–	1,496,000	–	1,792,000	97	77	104	96	95	97
UK	626,000	577,000	269,000	260,000	108	125	96	98	80	87
EU	–	8,923,000	–	8,644,000	120	125	101	101	107	–

Change in a manufacturing region: the Ruhr

We have seen that agriculture has undergone a series of changes that were due to several factors. Secondary industry, or manufacturing, has undergone similar changes. In this section we look at manufacturing at a regional scale.

▼ **Figure 5.13**
The Ruhr region.

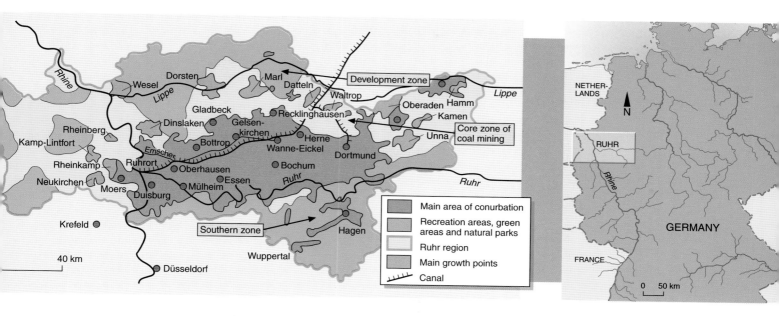

What and where is the Ruhr?

The Ruhr is an area in the German province of North Rhine Westphalia. It is a large industrial and urban area along the banks of the river Ruhr, and consists of a network of towns and cities with a total population of about 7.5 million. It is Europe's largest manufacturing industrial region (Figure 5.13).

The region has become famous for its coal and steel production, which continues now. Coal mining began in the area in the 1830s, but did not develop into a major industry until the 1870s when it was discovered that the coal here was suitable for coking coal, which is used in making iron and steel. This area then became one of the world's greatest centres for coal and for making steel.

The Ruhr region had several benefits:

- The raw materials for industry were found close together.

- The Ruhr is in the centre of the European continent.

- There are good, cheap transport routes through the region, along the river Rhine, and including two major canals.

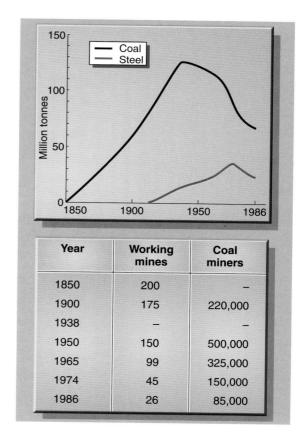

Year	Working mines	Coal miners
1850	200	–
1900	175	220,000
1938	–	–
1950	150	500,000
1965	99	325,000
1974	45	150,000
1986	26	85,000

▲ **Figure 5.14**
Coal and steel production in the Ruhr, 1850–1986.

a

b

▲ **Figure 5.15**
The Ruhr region: **a** *as it was 100 years ago, and* **b** *the Thyssen-Hochhaus building in the Ruhr today.*

This area has twice recovered from the devastation of world wars in the 20th century.

From the 1950s, coal production began to decline. This was a result of several factors:

- Oil began to compete with coal as a major source of energy.

- The mines in the south of the region were exhausted, and new mines in the north had to be much deeper in order to reach the coal. This made the coal much more expensive.

- Increasing mechanisation meant that fewer miners were needed.

The increase in the cost of coal also affected the cost of steel production in the region. At the same time, in other parts of the world, huge new coastal steelworks were being built which could produce steel more cheaply. In the 1970s and 1980s there was a fall in demand for steel products generally. Between the mid-1970s and the mid-1980s, steel production in the Ruhr region declined by almost one-third.

The changing industrial pattern

In the 1950s more than 60 per cent of all jobs in the region depended on coal and steel. Today only 30 per cent of workers are employed in these industries. The area has successfully managed to change its employment structure. Although the loss of so many mining jobs was painful to individuals, the Ruhr is still an area of great wealth and opportunity. There are four main reasons why the region has been so successful.

1 Restructuring of coal and steel

Steel companies concentrated their efforts on the most efficient and cost-effective sites. These were the ones on waterfront locations along rivers, which were able to take advantage of cheap water transport. Many companies amalgamated into larger companies in order to benefit from economies of scale. They also diversified into a wider range of products, and in 1997 the two largest companies – Krupp and Thyssen – seemed likely to merge into a single 'super-company'. They still produce steel, but they have also developed interests in industries that use steel. For example, they have offered their expertise in design to build complete factories for other companies (Figure 5.16).

a *A Krupp steel mill in Duisburg.*

Krupp	Thyssen
• Marine engineering • Electronic equipment • Coils and springs • Metal forging • Mechanical engineering • Plant construction • Making boilers and tanks • Diesel engines • Engineering and construction • Special steels • Machine tools	• Lifts and escalators • Iron and steel wire • Special steels • Vehicle components • Metals recycling • Plumbing materials • Machine tools • Shipbuilding • Design and construction • Oil production • Gas supply

b *A Thyssen factory in the Ruhr.*

2 Research and development

Companies in the area have placed great emphasis on research. The region includes 14 universities, and these have developed technology centres which link industry and the universities. This means that new ideas can quickly be turned into new products.

▲ **Figure 5.16**
Products of two Ruhr companies and their subsidiaries.

3 Pleasant environment

Politicians and planners, with the help of ordinary people, decided that it was important to create an attractive environment. Land that had been left derelict by industry was turned into parks. For an area of 7.5 million people, the Ruhr has exceptionally large areas of open space, and there are also facilities for walking, cycling and water sports.

▼ **Figure 5.17**
Land use in the Ruhr.

4 Location

Finally, the Ruhr region has taken particular advantage of its position in Europe. It advertises itself as being 'The Heart of Europe'. It has excellent communication links by rail, road and air. It also has an industrial structure that is 'linked' – that is, the factories in the region have many local customers. By using each other's products, firms can respond to each other's needs quickly, and cut down on transport costs and delivery times.

Total area	4,434 km^2
Agriculture	43.2%
Built-up area	21.5%
Woodland	17.3%
Roads	9.4%
Other	8.6%

Activities

1 Compose a case study of the Ruhr region of Germany. You should include:

- a sketch map to show the location and main features of the region

- a graph to show the changing nature of the coal and steel industries in the region

- notes on the industrial history of the region, describing its growth and decline.

2 Can you name any regions in the UK that have a similar history of growth and decline?

3 Put yourself in the shoes of a consultant for a declining industrial region in the UK. Use what you have found out about the Ruhr to advise on how to develop success in the future. In your report include notes on:

- how industry in the region was restructured

- the role played by universities in changing the area's industrial structure

- how the region used the environment to attract businesses

- how the region's location was used to help it attract new business.

Industrialisation and development: China

In the 19th century China was described as 'a sleeping giant', meaning that potentially it was a very powerful country, but at the time it was not using that potential. In the 1990s, once again, people are pointing to China as a country of enormous power, but this time they mean economically. While China is still regarded as a 'developing country', with 27 per cent of its workforce employed in agriculture, at the same time it is making rapid economic progress (Figure 5.18).

Until 1901 China was ruled by emperors who exercised complete power over the Chinese people. Between 1901 and 1939 China was in a state of almost permanent civil war, with various groups and warlords trying to seize power. During the Second World War the Japanese occupied the country, but once they were defeated, civil war broke out again. In 1949 the Communist forces were victorious, and Chairman Mao Zedong came to power. Nearly 50 years of fighting had left the country in a very poor state.

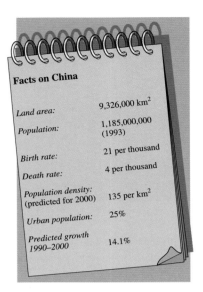

Facts on China

Land area:	9,326,000 km²
Population:	1,185,000,000 (1993)
Birth rate:	21 per thousand
Death rate:	4 per thousand
Population density: (predicted for 2000)	135 per km²
Urban population:	25%
Predicted growth 1990–2000	14.1%

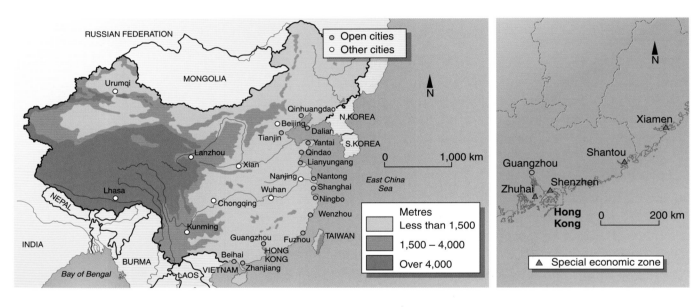

▲ **Figure 5.18**
Fact File: China.

The aim of the Communists was to create a better life for all the people. The state took control of all the land, factories and businesses. It controlled the whole economy. A series of five-year plans was established for industries. Each industry was set a target for production. In the early years the government concentrated on making steel and textiles, and mining coal, as these were needed for other industries and to meet people's needs. Steel was needed to build machines, railways and vehicles. Textiles were needed to clothe people, and coal was needed as a source of energy for industry.

In 1959 the government decided to increase the pace of development and launched 'The Great Leap Forward'. The plan stressed the need for people to work together. Instead of having their own land, families worked the village land together as a community, or commune. Each commune was set targets for production. The government also decided the wage levels. Communes were also encouraged to begin to make industrial products.

Production did increase, but bad management and poor organisation meant that transport links were not ready, food was left to rot on the communes, and many Chinese starved to death. Chairman Mao blamed the failure on managers and academics, and in 1966 tried to take even more control of the people through the disastrous period of 'The Cultural Revolution', when the managers and academics were themselves sent to work in the fields. Mao died in 1976, and the new leadership tried to develop new ideas.

In 1978 the government began to develop light industries, such as electrical goods and small machines. It also tried to increase production by allowing farms and factories more freedom to make their own decisions. China began to move towards what is called a market economy. It was thought that by allowing farmers and workers to make profits for themselves, this would increase production.

Year	Steel (million tonnes)	Coal (million tonnes)	Ships (thousand tonnes)	Watches (millions)	TVs (millions)
1949	0	32	0	0	0
1961	13	278	0	0	0
1970	21	354	0	4	0
1982	37	600	0	30	2.5
1990	66	1,078	340	86	25

◀ **Figure 5.19**
China's industrial development, 1949–90.

In the mid-1990s this idea was taken a stage further with the creation of Special Economic Zones (SEZs) and 'open cities' (see Figure 5.18). These are areas of the country which are allowed to attract foreign companies to set up factories there. This meant that foreign companies now had access to Chinese markets, in an area where wages and production costs were particularly low. China benefits from this arrangement by earning money from abroad, and increasing the skills of its workforce.

Routes to development

For any developing country there are limited options available when trying to develop the industrial structure.

1 Borrow money to build factories.

2 Use the money made from selling primary products to build factories.

3 Attract transnational companies (TNCs) to invest in the country.

4 Develop a tourist industry.

Each of these measures has its drawbacks. The problem with option 1 is that the money has to be repaid with interest. Many countries, such as Brazil and Mexico, have borrowed so much money that they are finding it very difficult to repay their debts.

China's new age entrepreneurs

Women in Guangzhou are making the most of the new business opportunities in southern China, **Linda Yeung** discovers

Women have always been a dominant force in China, making up close to half of the total employees. And now, with the country's economy taking off, especially in the south, many have ventured into far more ambitious pursuits.

Women's entrepreneurs' associations have sprung up in boom towns such as Guangzhou and Zhuhai.

Fifty-year-old Chen Huimei, a mother of two teenage children, is not a member, but archetypal of the newly emerged, driven women entrepreneurs.

Ms Chen's business had a turnover of between 3 million yuan (about US $360,000) to 4 million yuan last year.

It is a far cry from the home-based mechanical processing and repair business she established with her mechanic husband in the early 1980s, starting with a capital of just 300 yuan.

'The metal factory I was working for at that time was on the verge of collapse,' she recalled in a plain office in her retail outlet, less than half-an-hour's drive away from the centre of Guangzhou.

The success story began when she and her husband were presented with a broken air-inlet pipe used for a car air-conditioning system one day.

'That was not made in China. No one here made it then,' said Ms Chen.

Their present factory, sited in a more distant location where her husband is based, now employs 38 staff.

From the
South China Morning Post

Zhou Wei manages a department store in the prosperous eastern Chinese city of Wuxi, and lives in a new three-storey townhouse.

Wang Baocai raises goats in Zhujiagou Village, 950 km away in north-central China. He lives in a cave.

Despite the stark contrast in living conditions, Ms Zhou and Mr Wang have prospered during the 16 years of economic liberalisation since senior leader Deng Xiaoping took power and turned Maoism on its head.

Mr Wang, 46, freed from collective farming by the economic reforms, manages a herd of 40 goats and last year made nearly US $900 for his seven-member household. Two black-and-white television sets flicker in his home dug into the yellow earth of Shaanxi Province.

'Before reforms none of this would have been possible,' said Wang, motioning proudly towards his modest hillside property. 'Fifteen years ago we did not have enough to eat. No one could own private goats.'

But Ms Zhou, a stout 47-year-old woman who manages the 'Island of Dreams Shopping Centre' in Wuxi, a bustling lake city north-west of Shanghai, has benefited even more. She owns several homes, a Dodge caravan, and takes home US $2,500 a month – more than 30 times Mr Wang's income.

From the *Hong Kong Standard*, 22 July 1995

▲ **Figure 5.20**

Aspects of modern China.

In relation to option 2, China has such a large population that it has found it difficult to sell its raw materials abroad because they are needed to feed, house and clothe its own people.

TNCs create jobs and use local raw materials. They also create jobs in factories that supply components, and they increase the skill levels of local workers. However, profits return to the parent company in another country. The TNC can also decide to leave at any time, and so this is not a stable basis for a country's economic development.

China has now begun to develop its own tourist industry – this route to development is considered later in this unit. One drawback for China is that tourists import 'Western' ideas, beliefs and practices, which the authorities consider are unhealthy for the development of the Chinese nation.

China has a reputation for being cut off from the rest of the world, and for not welcoming outside interference. Many people were surprised when it created the SEZs.

Chinese success?

We can judge if a country is developing economically by looking at its changing industrial structure and by looking at the products a country imports and exports. We would expect a country to begin to export fewer raw materials and more manufactured goods as it develops economically. Figure 5.21 will help you to decide whether economic development has taken place in China.

	1985		1990	
	Imports	Exports	Imports	Exports
Food & live animals	3.6	1.4	6.5	10.8
Beverages & tobacco	0.5	0.4	0.3	0.6
Inedible raw materials	7.6	9.7	7.7	5.7
Mineral fuels	0.4	25.9	2.4	8.4
Animal & vegetable oils	0.3	0.5	1.8	0
Chemicals	10.4	5.0	12.5	6.0
Manufactured goods	27.9	16.5	21.7	20.6
Machinery & transport	38.9	2.8	40.3	17.4
Miscellaneous manufacturing	4.5	12.8	6.2	28.2
Miscellaneous transport	5.9	12.4	0.5	1.9
Others	-	12.6	0.1	0.4

◀ **Figure 5.21**
Trade in China: percentage of total imports and exports, 1985 and 1990.

▼ **Figure 5.22**   *The Pacific Rim.*

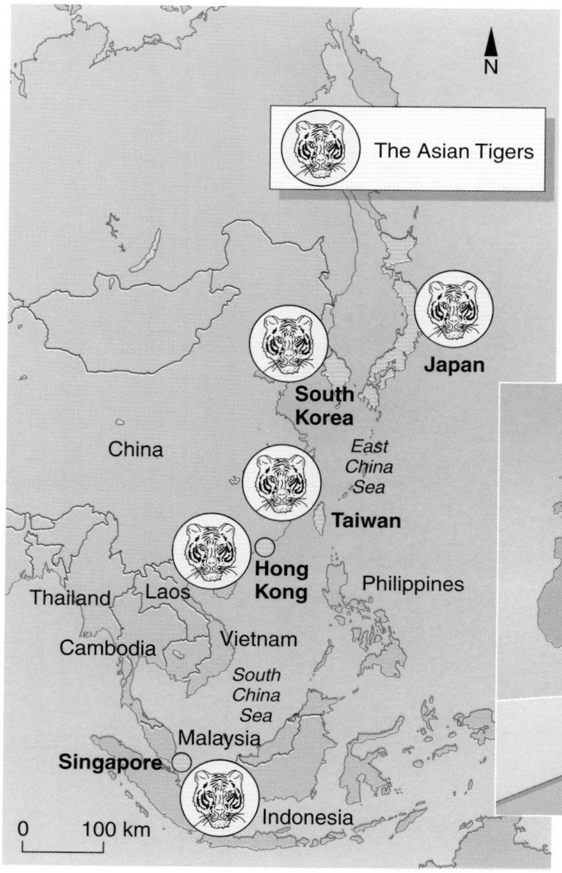

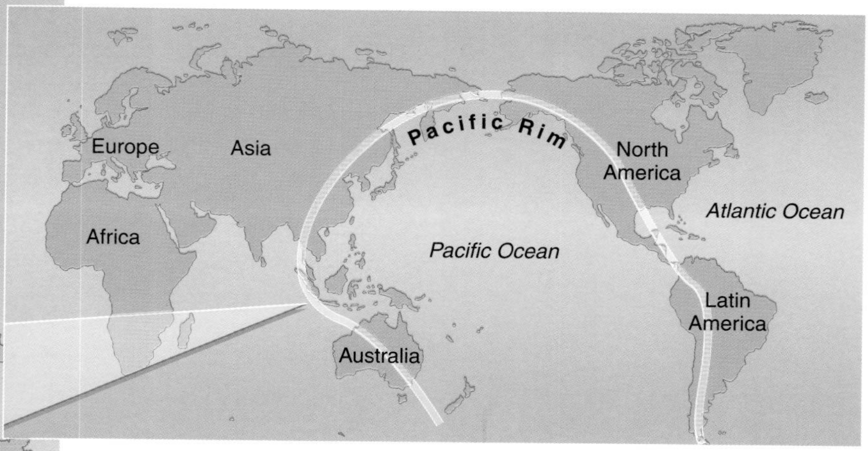

The Pacific Rim

As with the Ruhr, China benefits from its location. Throughout the 1990s the idea of the 'Pacific Rim' has been growing. The term refers to the 'tiger economies' that lie around the Pacific Ocean (Figure 5.22). The tiger economies are countries like Japan, Taiwan and South Korea, which have transformed themselves into competitive and leading trading nations. Figure 5.23 shows how Asian countries top the economic growth league table. The Pacific is set to become a new world industrial region (the USA and Europe are the others).

All good news?

As we have already seen, however, development is not only concerned with the creation of wealth. It also reflects the distribution of wealth and the well-being of the population. There is no doubt that China has developed its ability to create wealth. It also has a much more even distribution of wealth than many other countries. However, there is much concern over the issue of human rights in China since the government there crushed demonstrations against the Communist regime in the early 1990s. Although many countries have expressed their concern, even nations as powerful as the USA have backed away from voicing their opinions too strongly. Perhaps they realise that the sleeping giant has begun to stir – trade with a country the size of China could bring economic benefits to other people all over the world. Possibly the greatest concern should be about the environmental damage that can be caused by a country without any 'people power' (democracy), intent on economic growth at any cost.

▶ **Figure 5.23**
Economic growth rates of selected countries, 1980–88.

World ranking	Country	% growth rate
1	China	11.4
2	Botswana	10.6
3	Oman	9.8
4	Laos	9.1
5	South Korea	9.0
6	Bhutan	8.1
7	North Yemen	8.0
8	Macao	7.7
9	Hong Kong	7.6
10	Taiwan	7.5
57	UK	2.8

Activities

1 Compose a case study of China. You could include all or some of the following:

- A sketch map to show

  - Beijing

  - the SEZs and the 'open cities'

  - the main rivers

  - the relief (the main upland areas).

- Notes listing the main events in China's 20th-century history.

- A description of changes since the death of Mao. (For example, you could describe how the lives of the three people in **Figure 5.20** have changed as a result of the new policies in China.)

2 You are a journalist for a local newspaper's 'Business Page'. You've been asked to write 250 words on the Pacific Rim in order to inform readers about the economic success of the 'tiger economies'. Use facts and figures where necessary to explain this success. You could ask your teachers and other adults why they think countries like Singapore and South Korea are economically so successful.

Tourism: a tertiary industry

Tertiary industries are those that supply services rather than make products. They have become increasingly important in the last 30 years all over the world. This section looks at tourism as an example of a tertiary industry. It concentrates on a country that is seeking to use its natural beauty to develop a thriving tertiary sector, and considers how the demands of tourism may conflict with the need to protect vulnerable environments.

Tourism worldwide

Tourism generates between 3.5 and 4 trillion dollars each year. It is estimated that it employs 30 million of the world's population, or 1 in every 15 workers. It is the world's single most important earner of foreign currency.

Many countries have sought to develop their tourist industry because it is cheaper to set up than many other industries. It also repays investment in a shorter period of time. Build a hotel and in come the tourists to spend money! This is a simple formula that does not always work, but for every 30 new tourists one 'direct' job and two 'indirect' jobs are created. It also leads to the development of infrastructure such as roads, energy and communications networks, and leisure facilities for everyone.

Tourism in South Africa

▼ **Figure 5.24**
South Africa.

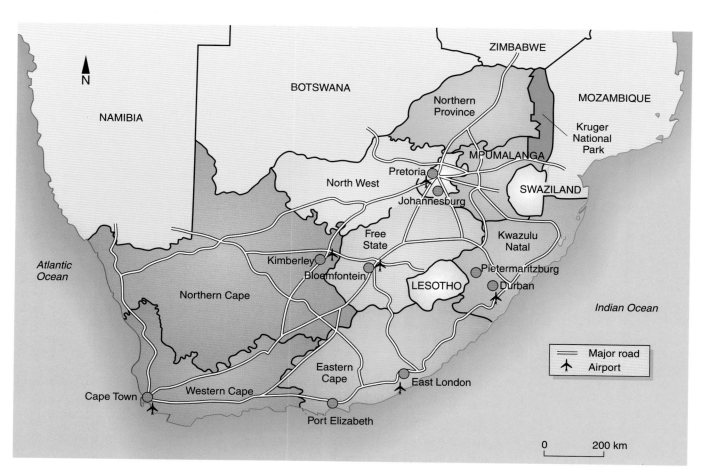

Year	Number of overseas visitors
1975	402,988
1976	362,280
1977	302,247
1978	337,042
1979	377,911
1980	404,391
1981	446,112
1982	389,155
1983	405,414
1984	454,880
1985	405,597
1986	297,060
1987	339,307
1988	388,102
1989	472,076
1990	498,712
1991	521,257
1992	559,913
1993	618,508
1994	704,630

▲ **Figure 5.25**
Visitors to South Africa, 1975–94.

• Scenic beauty	23.0%
• Wildlife	21.7%
• Sunny climate	11.5%
• African culture	7.8%
• Diversity of attractions	7.1%
• Value for money	4.4%

▲ **Figure 5.26**
What are South Africa's main attractions? Results of a questionnaire issued to foreign visitors.

At present tourism employs 450,000 people in South Africa and earns 3 per cent of the country's GNP. It is the fourth largest earner of foreign currency. Figure 5.25 shows the growth of tourism between 1975 and 1994. In 1995 the number of visitors to South Africa rose by 50 per cent, making it the fastest-growing tourist destination in the world.

Until 1994 South Africa operated a racist political system known as 'apartheid', or 'separate development'. In practice this meant that the white people, who are in the minority, controlled the country, while the larger black population had no power. Most other countries disapproved of the system, and would not trade with South Africa. Many people refused to buy South African products or to visit the country. However, after the peaceful abolition of the apartheid system and with the election of President Nelson Mandela, South Africa was welcomed back into the international trading community. It has begun to restructure the country for the benefit of all its citizens, and tourists are strongly encouraged to visit the country.

Developing South Africa's potential

South Africa is very proud of its physical environment. The results of a survey in which foreign visitors were asked about the main attractions of the country are presented in Figure 5.26.

On the basis of this information, the South African Tourist Authority (SATOUR) decided to promote four particular aspects of the country:

- spectacular scenic beauty

- cultural diversity

- wildlife

- sophisticated infrastructure.

Eco-tourism

'Eco-tourism' can be defined as:

- purposeful travel to natural areas to understand the culture and natural history of the environment

- producing economic opportunities that can conserve the natural resources of the area for the benefit of local people.

Examples of eco-tourism include birdwatching, nature photography, painting, snorkelling, hiking and mountain climbing.

South Africa has 16 National Parks and one National Lake Area, with a total land area of 3.2 million hectares. There are 4,300 people employed in these special areas. The most famous is the Kruger National Park, which covers nearly 20,000 km^2. It has over 140 species of mammal and 450 bird species. The government and SATOUR are determined to develop a tourist industry that:

a *Cape South Africa.*

Figure 5.27
South Africa's special attractions.

b *People of the Zulu tribe.*

c *South African sunbird.*

d *Cape Town.*

- is environmentally friendly

- benefits companies, workers and the local community

- develops a sense of responsibility for the environment.

The future

Latest estimates predict rapid growth for the tourist industry in South Africa. Whilst this will obviously help the economy, there are several hazards, such as unsuitable development, over-use of certain areas, and the destruction of the local way of life.

Activities

1 Why is tourism an important industry around the globe?

2 Why do many countries choose tourism as a means of developing their industrial structure?

3 Draw a graph to show the increase in tourism in South Africa between 1980 and 1994. Describe any trends revealed by your graph.

4 a 'Thirty tourists provide one "direct" and two "indirect" jobs.' Think carefully about this statement, and write two lists: one of **direct** jobs, and the other of **indirect** jobs resulting from tourism.

b For each job you have identified, state whether the job would be located in the country of origin of the tourists, or the country of destination.

5 Think about the development of eco-tourism in South Africa over the next ten years. Will it be possible for the government to create an industry that meets all its aims?

a Write two descriptions of what effects you think the tourist industry could have on the country. Call one description 'The ideal future' and the other 'The probable future'.

b If your two accounts are different, what is the main **reason** for the difference?

Too many tourists?

To show the effects that large numbers of tourists can have on an area, this section looks at the Snowdonia National Park in north Wales.

What are the main aims of Snowdonia National Park?

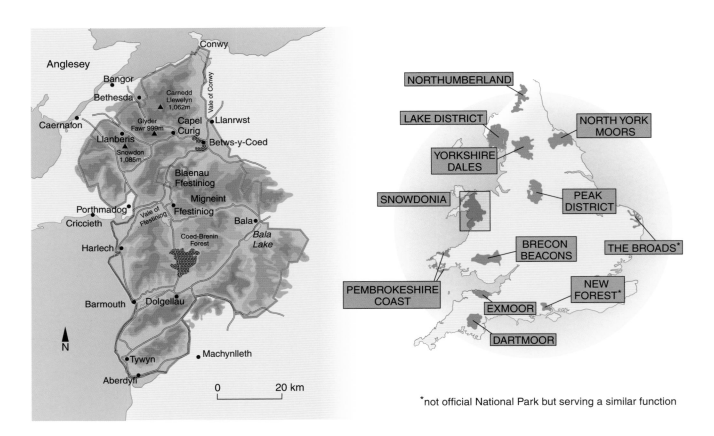

*not official National Park but serving a similar function

▲ **Figure 5.28**

The National Parks of England and Wales, and Snowdonia National Park.

Snowdonia National Park was created in 1951. Its main aims were – and still are – to conserve the beauty of the countryside and to manage the environment so that people can be encouraged to visit the area. These aims conflict with each other.

What is Snowdonia like?

The Park has an area of 2,155 km². Much of the scenery has been shaped by glaciation. It has several ranges of high, craggy mountains, including the highest, Snowdon. There are large areas of bleak moorland, some of it now covered by coniferous forest. The park includes a stretch of coastline and three large river estuaries.

Most of the 25,000 people who live in the Park are Welsh, and Welsh is used as the everyday first language. The people live in villages or small towns clustered in sheltered valleys. Large numbers of tourists – equal to 10 million visitor-days each year – visit the Park but they tend to cluster at 'honeypot' sites such as Snowdon. Some parts of the Park attract very few tourists. The following describes the Migneint, a bleak, unspectacular part of the park where there are not many tourists.

The impact of tourists

The increasing numbers of tourists have damaged the Park's highest mountain, but the Park authorities are trying to deal with the problem.

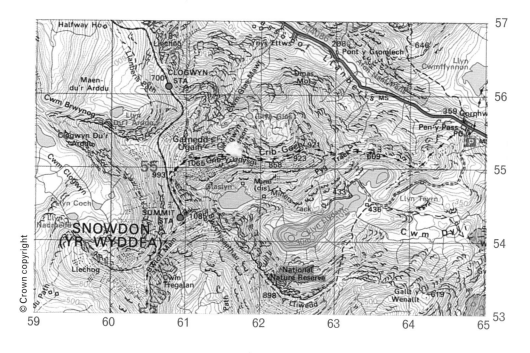

© Crown copyright

▲ **Figure 5.29**
Aspects of Snowdonia.

a   *The Aberglaslyn Pass. This vertically-sided gorge was cut by the power of a melting glacier. It is one of the main tourist attractions.*

b   *Harlech Castle. Built in 1290 by Edward I, this is one of several castles guarding the north Wales coast.*

c   *Llynnau Mymbyr, with Snowdon beyond. There are several 'ribbon' lakes in the Park which were formed by glaciers. Some of these lakes are now used for windsurfing and sailing. There has been a steady increase in adventure-style holidays.*

◄ **Figure 5.30**
Extract from the OS 1:50 000 map sheet 115 of the Snowdon area.

Unit 5 **Economic Activity and the Geography of Development**

▲ Figure 5.31

The summit of Snowdon. There is a railway station – the terminus of the Snowdon Mountain Railway – and a café at the top of the mountain.

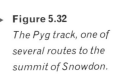

▶ Figure 5.32

The Pyg track, one of several routes to the summit of Snowdon.

Conflict in the Park

The National Park lies partly in the Gwynedd County Council area. The Council has a wide range of responsibilities which can conflict with those of the National Park. Local people and environmentalists often disagree as to whether developments such as a new road or a large hotel should be allowed to go ahead. Some towns and villages which relied on slate mining have declined. Emigration, particularly by people in the younger age groups, is a problem. The Council wants to help the economy of the area by improving accessibility.

Activities

1 Make a list of the words describing the variety of scenery in Snowdonia. From your analysis of these, what do you consider are the main scenic attractions of the National Park?

2 a Why are some parts of the Park particularly popular with tourists (honeypots) while other areas are hardly visited?

 b What are the advantages to the National Park authorities of encouraging people to honeypots? (*Hint:* How can this policy help solve the conflicting aims of conserving the landscape, and encouraging tourism?)

3 Sally Gillman regrets that Snowdon became too popular (**Figure 5.33**). Put forward an argument against Sally, explaining why access to the mountain should be improved.

Sally Gillman

I first climbed Snowdon 30 years ago, when I was 8 years old. It was an exciting adventure to climb to the top of the steep, sharp peak. It was a sunny August day, but we hardly met anyone on the way. I was astonished to see a railway at the top. I thought it should not be there and it spoiled my feeling of achievement. I wanted to be alone on this remote mountain top. The station included a tatty café, although it did serve delicious cocoa. I climbed Snowdon last February, in gale-force winds. Even though it was an unpleasant day the car park at Pen-y-Pass was full. I was shocked to see how much the mountain had changed since my first visit. Eroded footpaths scarred the mountainside. Paths had been made up to a smooth surface and it was like walking on a pavement. It seems as if people are being encouraged to go up in sandals! The final steep section had been cut into steps so there was no need to scramble any more. I want to share my enjoyment of the mountains with other people, but it is a shame when a place of beauty becomes spoilt, either by footpath erosion or by very obvious repairs.

David Archer, National Park Officer

As many as 250,000 people reach the top of Snowdon each year, 150,000 having walked, the others using the railway. This fragile and exposed mountain top is more heavily trampled than some city pavements. All the footpaths are eroded, especially the two most popular ones. Erosion is triggered when repeated trampling kills fragile plants. Without plants to protect the soil by intercepting the heavy rainfall, water runs down the slope at speed, taking some of the soil with it. Stone is soon exposed and most people then walk on the grass on either side of the path. The process repeats itself, making the path increasingly wider. We have repaired large sections of the paths on Snowdon, although we haven't got the finances to begin work on other damaged mountains. Our surfaced paths have been criticised for not looking natural. On other eroded paths local stone has been pitched into the ground to form a stone walkway. Conservationists prefer this as after a few years the stone looks like an old packhorse route. We have improved the car park at Pen-y-Pass but deliberately kept its size down to 130 spaces. By imposing parking restrictions on the approach roads we hope to control the number of people walking on the Pyg and Miner's tracks. This will always be a heavily used mountain but there are several routes to the top. Litter is not really a problem on the mountain tops, as most walkers seem environmentally aware. However, casual visitors who stop for a picnic without leaving the car park area do cause us concern. We've installed large rubbish skips which are emptied several times a week. We encourage the 'park and ride' scheme between Pen-y-Pass and Llanberis, which operates in summer. It helps local businesses and takes pressure off the most congested roads.

Values

National Parks came into being in 1951 because the government believed the landscapes in these areas (see Figure 5.28) were valued highly. It was worth conserving these areas for the benefit of everyone. However, individual opinions vary, as Figure 5.33 shows.

▲ **Figure 5.33**
Using and caring for the Park.

Activities

1 Analyse the statements by Sally Gillman and David Archer, in terms of their *values*. Look for *what* they say, and *how* they say it.

2 Sally is an individual looking for recreation. David is an individual whose job it is to manage the Park for everyone. How do their different *perspectives* influence what they value?

THINKING GEOGRAPHY

The European dimension

What is the European Union?

At the end of the Second World War, European leaders wanted to avoid the continent being torn apart by war again. The idea was developed to try to promote greater political, economic and cultural unity among the nations of Europe. The European Economic Community (EEC) was created in 1957 with six nations, and by 1994 the number of countries involved had increased to fifteen. This group has changed its name several times to show a gradual change in emphasis from many economic links to greater political co-operation. It began life as the European Economic Community. This was changed to the European Community (EC) and then in 1994 to the European Union (EU).

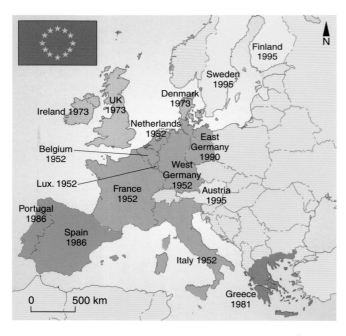

▲ *Development of the European Union.*

What is the aim of the EU?

To create a single region in which goods, services, people and money can move as freely as within individual countries.

How is it run?

The EU is managed by six organisations (see below). Decisions are made by the Council of Ministers. This is made up of ministers from each of the member countries. Proposals made by them are discussed by the European Parliament in Strasbourg, and changes can be suggested. Final proposals are then put into practice by the European Commission in Brussels.

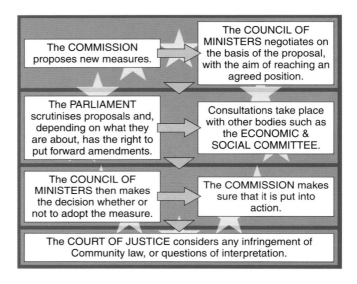

▲ *The organisation of the European Union.*

How is the EU financed?

EU funds come from four sources:

VAT Countries pay up to 1.4% of the money they collect from VAT into European funds.

Customs duties The EU taxes products from other parts of the world.

Agricultural levies The Union also taxes agricultural products from other parts of the world.

National contributions Each country negotiates an amount of money to pay into the European budget. Generally, the rich countries pay more than the poorer ones.

Thinking Geography **The European dimension**

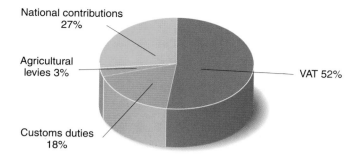

National contributions 27%

Agricultural levies 3%

VAT 52%

Customs duties 18%

▲ *How the EU gets its money.*

How does the EU spend its money?

The areas in which the EU spends its money are as follows:

1 Agriculture and fishing – subsidising food production

2 Regional expenditure – this consists of grants to develop poorer areas of the EU

3 Social expenditure – training, resettlement and job creation

4 Research, industry, energy and environmental policies

5 Overseas aid

6 Administration

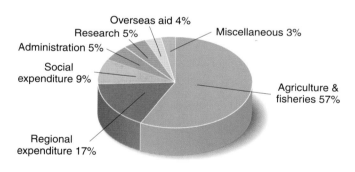

Overseas aid 4%

Research 5%

Administration 5%

Social expenditure 9%

Miscellaneous 3%

Agriculture & fisheries 57%

Regional expenditure 17%

▲ *How the EU spends its money.*

How may membership of the EU affect you?

If the EU is to achieve its aim it may change many aspects of your life. For instance, the next development is the introduction of a single currency. This would mean that instead of using pounds or pesetas, for example, all the countries of the EU would use just one unit, the Euro. The discussions around this idea highlight the difference of opinion about the aims of the EU.

The use of one currency would make it much easier to trade in Europe. It would also make travel much easier. However, it would also mean that more decisions would have to be made by the Council of Ministers, and fewer by national governments. Some people see this as a good thing and are keen to develop more European integration. Others feel that a single currency would weaken national independence. Some Germans find it difficult to accept Germany without the Deutschmark, and many British will not easily accept Britain without the pound. They feel that countries should co-operate economically but should not lose their individual identities.

Over the next few years other countries are expected to join the European Union, such as Poland, Hungary and Turkey. It will be one of the world's largest trade blocks. Inside the EU there will be freedom of movement and an open market for all European goods. Outside the Union people will have to pay duties to sell their goods to Europeans. The Council of Ministers will make decisions for perhaps 400 million people. They must ensure that their decisions reflect the needs of all of Europe's diverse peoples and regions.

Activities

Draw up a personal European 'balance sheet'. To do this, first consider the EU as an idea, and secondly as an impact on your life.

1 List reasons **a** why the EU is a good idea and **b** why it is not a good idea.

2 List ways in which you believe the EU has directly benefited you and your family. List ways you feel the EU has had a negative impact on your life.

3 Identify geographical and historical reasons why:

   a Germany is a nation that is usually strongly in favour of European integration

   b Britain has a more sceptical outlook on European integration.

4 If a British government gave you the chance to vote for or against remaining part of the EU, how would you vote? Write a memo researching your reasons. Date it, sign it, and keep it: it may be interesting to see how your views change as you grow older.

Preparing for the exams

An important aim during the two years of your GCSE course is to achieve the highest possible grade. To do this you must try to strike a balance between the different ways in which you will be assessed.

Coursework

During the course you will have to complete coursework. An essential way of ensuring good marks here is to complete the work on time. You must make sure you know how your work will be marked. It is important that you allow the person marking your work to reward your efforts. They can only do this if you present your work in the correct way and stick to the point. Very few marks will be awarded for large sections copied from textbooks or CD-ROMs. To earn marks, photographs, maps and graphs must be linked into the study and explained. You need to make sure that you:

set the scene	say what your work sets out to achieve and how you aim to do this
describe	say what you have found
explain	say why it is like this
offer conclusions	sum up why it is important, and suggest what might happen in the future; consider other things that could have helped your study.

The final exams

It is important to remember that the exam will include work on topics that you studied right at the beginning of your course. It's a good idea to go back through your work at regular intervals. Read through what you have written to identify and remember the key points.

Some myths about exams

1 *Failure will ruin your life*

   Failing an exam is not the end of the world, so keep your anxieties in proper proportion.

2 *The exam could expose you as a fool and a fraud*

   Everyone wants you to pass, including the examiner.

3 *You should have read everything in the course before attempting the exam*

Don't worry about what you *haven't* done during your course. Work out how to make the best use of what you *have* done.

4 *If you haven't understood what you've read there's no point taking the exam*

No one understands everything. There are bound to be areas where you feel less well prepared or confused. Talking with friends can help. In the end you do your best, which is often better than you think.

5 *Exams are for people with a good memory*

It's a matter of how you use it. Exams tend to be about what you *understand* rather than what you can *remember*. Getting your course notes organised is important. If your understanding is sound and the work well organised, remembering usually happens automatically.

6 *Exams are just for speed merchants*

What matters is how well you've organised your ideas and how well you've planned your exam strategy. 'Speed' in an exam is to do with having a clear plan of how you intend to use your time.

7 *Before an exam you need to revise until you drop*

You will probably do a lot of work just before the exam. But you need to do it in a planned way, using your time efficiently and conserving your energies. You don't want to turn your life into a complete misery just because of an exam. A little bit often, rather than hours at a time, is advisable.

What's the point of revision?

The most important aim of revision is to pull together all the work you've done in studying your course. It's not really a memory task. The more constructive it is the more useful it will be. For Geography exams you need to try to link ideas together. As in coursework you are asked to *describe*, *explain* and *draw conclusions*.

Organising your revision

Understanding questions

During the course you should have attempted several GCSE questions and have completed mock exams. You know what exam questions are like but it's worthwhile trying to understand the *structure* of the exam questions. They often fall into three sections. Look at the exam question on pages 160–162, about employment differences between a more economically developed country and a less economically developed country. You are asked to do three things.

1 *Respond to data*

In the question you're given two population pyramids to study. You have to add information to them and select information from them. The data you are asked to respond to might be a map or photo. It might be a graph or a pie chart. It will probably be about a place you have not studied, but it will be about an idea that you have explored. This is usually the easiest part of the question, and the answers are all to be found in the information provided.

2 *Go deeper*

Having raised the subject with you, the examiner wants to find out how well you understand it. Often you will be asked to describe patterns or explain why something happens. You may be asked how it would affect different groups of people or countries.

3 *Show what you know*

The last section is usually called the *case study*. You are asked to write about a place you have studied. You will probably have a case study for each idea that you have studied in the course. It's very important to pick a case study that fits the question. You must read the question carefully and make sure your example is correct. In our example, for instance, you're asked to write about employment structures in a less economically developed country.

Activities

1 Give an example from this book that you could use as a case study for the examination question shown on page 162.

2 Have a look at the other questions included in this book. Try to split them into the three sections of a typical exam question.

3 Now have a go at writing your own exam question.

    a Find a map or graph that relates to a topic you have studied.

    b *Respond to the data*. Make up some questions which ask for a response to the data you have provided.

    c *Go deeper*. Decide which geographical terms and patterns would need to be explained. Design questions that ask to show understanding of process and patterns.

    d *Show what you know*. Decide on a case study that would be suitable to end the question. Design the question that asks for knowledge of such a case study.

4 When you have written your question you can swap with someone else; try to answer their question.

Geography vocabulary

In the exam you will be asked to explain the meanings of words used in the course. The Glossary on pages 165–169 is designed to help you. It is quite easy to test yourself on these words. You could work with others asking for the meaning of a word. You could give the meaning and ask for the word. You could make up a multiple-choice question. The other important thing to remember about these words is that the more you use them in your answers, the higher the marks you will score. Try to use the correct words whenever possible. You might want to sort the Glossary into separate lists for each unit of work that you have studied.

Examiner's use of words

In the exam paper the examiner asks you to do various things, for example *describe, explain* or *compare*. You must make sure that you understand what each word means. Here is a chart of the most commonly used words, with the meaning and a possible answer.

Word *Study*	**Word** *Complete*	**Word** *List/Give*	**Word** *Describe*
Meaning Look closely at	**Meaning** Fill in or finish	**Meaning** Normally you will have to look at a map or picture and find out some information.	**Meaning** You will have to write about what you see on a map or photo. Try to use geographical terms such as north, south, central, clustered, dispersed.
Example 'Study the map on page 0.' (This is to make sure you know where to find the information you need.)	**Example** 'Complete the graph on page 0 by using the figures in chart Y.'	**Example** 'Give reasons why a superstore has been located at X.'	**Example** 'Describe the location of the Special Economic Zone.'
		Answer 'The superstore is accessible because it is near the junction of the A13 and the M25.'	**Answer** 'The Special Economic Zone is on the southern coast of China. It is approximately 150 kilometres to the north-west of Hong Kong.'

Word *Explain/Give reasons for/ Account for*	**Word** *Compare*	**Word** *Suggest*
Meaning You will be expected to say *why* something happens. You are usually asked to give two or three reasons.	**Meaning** You will be asked to say how two places are either *the same* or *different*.	**Meaning** Try to explain why something happens.
Example 'Give two reasons why London has many jobs in the tertiary sector.'	**Example** 'Compare the industrial structure of the UK and China.'	**Example** 'Suggest why so many old people live in the terraced houses of the city centre.'
Answer 'London has many jobs in the tertiary sector because it is the centre of government and there are many government offices there. Many large companies also have their head offices in London.'	**Answer** 'The UK has little primary industry but quite a lot of secondary and tertiary industry. China has more primary industry than the UK and less secondary and tertiary industry.'	**Answer** 'It might be because the houses are small and cheap to run. It might be that they are close to the shops of the city centre. Some people will have lived there all their lives and will not want to move.'

Case studies

By the end of two years your work folder will be very full. You will have lots of case studies. You need to be able to sort them out. Here are two ideas that might help you.

Revision cards

Many schools use this idea. For each of your named examples prepare a small card which summarises all you know about the topic.

It should include the following.

- The key ideas.
- A sketch map.
- Important geographical words – an example is shown below.

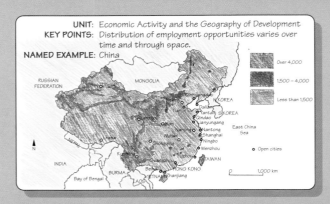

UNIT: Economic Activity and the Geography of Development
KEY POINTS: Distribution of employment opportunities varies over time and through space.
NAMED EXAMPLE: China

Over 4,000
1,500 – 4,000
Less than 1,500

○ Open cities

0   1,000 km

RUSSIAN FEDERATION
MONGOLIA
N KOREA
S KOREA
Dalian
Yantai
Qindao
Lianyungang
Nantong
Shanghai
Ningbo
Wenzhou
Fuzhou
TAIWAN
East China Sea
Guangzhou
Beihai
HONG KONG
VIETNAM Zhanjiang
NEPAL
INDIA
BURMA
LAOS
Bay of Bengal
N

MAIN POINTS
- After 1949 Communist Revolution China concentrated on producing food, steel, textiles and coal.
- Great Leap Forward tried to increase productivity but failed.
- In 1978 government began to develop light industry such as electrical goods.
- Government also allowed people to retain profits.
- 1990 saw introduction of Special Economic Zones – open cities designed to attract foreign investment.
- China had fastest economic growth rate in world between 1980 and 1988 – 11.4%.

Disadvantages
- Will benefits reach all?
- What will be the cost to the environment?

Key vocabulary
Communists, Special Economic Zones, growth rate

A key points grid

All the key points for a unit or section are written into a diamond grid, and these are then used to write a summary case study. Try transferring the points in this example onto a copy of the diamond diagram, putting the points into a logical order. (Some of these points are not related, and they are to 'catch you out'.) Once you've completed the diagram, write an outline case study. You can use each point/idea on the grid more than once.

Quality of life is relative

Average earnings	Inner city	Quality of life is relative	Unemployment
Quality of life can be measured	Quality of life in an area can change	Example of a UK city	High birth rate
Outer city	Quality of life improves as you move outwards through UK cities	Indicators are used to measure quality of life	Cool temperate climate
Car ownership	Lower quality of life	Inward investment by TNCs	Scale can hide differences
Lack of top carnivores	Quality of life varies between people in the same area	Wealth	Higher quality of life

Activities

1 Use your notes and this textbook to draw up a revision card for one idea covered by your course.

2 Make up a key points grid for each unit of this book.

On the big day

Having spent two years working and a long time planning, it is important to make the best use of your time on the day.

1 Make sure you know how many questions you must answer.

2 Read through the whole paper and decide which questions you are going to choose.

3 Double-check that your case study is suitable for the last part of the question.

4 Do the question on which you think you will score the most marks first, then the second best and so on.

5 Keep your eye on the time. Try to finish every question.

6 Don't waste valuable time worrying over an answer that will gain you only one mark.

7 Look out for places where the examiner is trying to help you. Read the titles of maps and graphs. Think about the words that are printed in **bold** type. Both these things are saying to you: 'Make sure you notice this'.

8 Make sure you use up all the time available. If you finish early, check your answers. If you have a lot of gaps, you can always have a guess at the answer.

Specimen exam papers

1 Foundation tier

(a) Study the graphs below. They show the population in a more economically developed country and a less economically developed country.

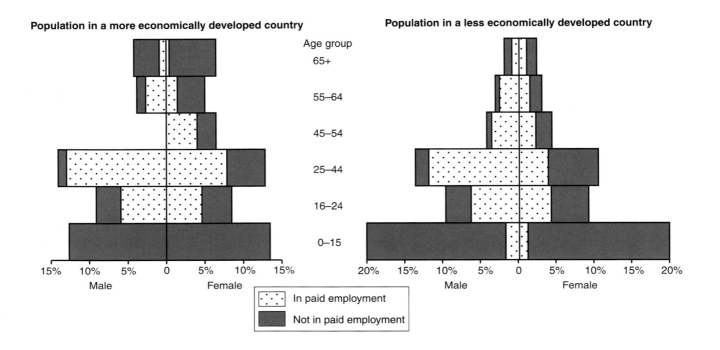

Population in a more economically developed country

Population in a less economically developed country

In paid employment

Not in paid employment

(i) Finish the graph by adding the information.

Country	Age group	Sex	% in paid employment	% not in paid employment
More economically developed	45–54	Male	5%	2%

[2]

(ii) For women aged 25–44 in the more economically developed country, what is the percentage for those in paid employment?

[1]

(iii) **Describe** how the two countries are different in terms of:
1 employment in the 0–15 age range
2 the proportion of people **not** in paid employment after the age of 65
3 the proportion of men and women in paid employment.

[6]

(iv) **Explain** why the two countries are different in terms of:
   1 employment in the 0–15 age range
   2 the percentage of people not in paid employment after the
      age of 65.   [4]

(v) **Compare** the two countries in terms of the **total** proportions of
     people in paid and not in paid employment.   [2]

(b) Study the map below. It shows the percentage of all paid workers in
     African countries who are women.

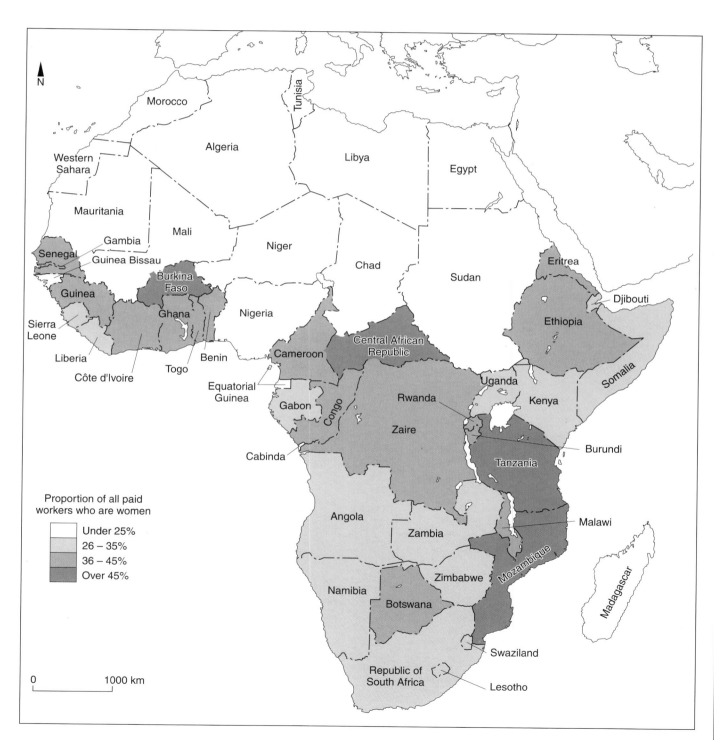

Proportion of all paid
workers who are women

- Under 25%
- 26 – 35%
- 36 – 45%
- Over 45%

0   1000 km

(i) In Nigeria the percentage (%) of paid workers who are women is 31%. Show this on the map. [1]

(ii) **Describe** the distribution of countries in which women are less than 35% of all paid workers. [3]

(iii) Suggest **three** reasons why the proportion of women in paid employment varies from one country to another. [6]

(c) **CASE STUDY**

The pie graph below shows the employment structure of the UK.

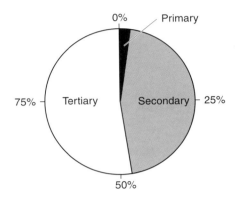

(i) How would the employment structure be different for a less economically developed country?

(ii) **Explain** the differences you have described in (c)(i). [5]

MEG Specimen exam paper prepared in 1996 for the 1998 examination

2 Higher tier

(a) Study this sketch map of a tourist area in mountains.

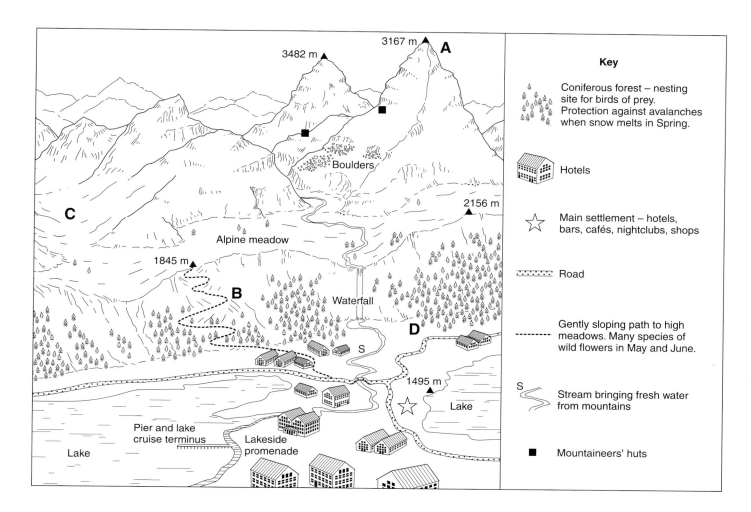

Using this information:

(i) The letters **A to D** on the sketch map show different areas of the
     mountains. Match each letter to **one** of the descriptions in the
     table below. (The first one has been done for you.)

DESCRIPTION OF AREA	LETTER
An area of fairly flat land lower than its surroundings	**D**
A steep mountain	....
A steep slope on one side of a large valley with lakes in it	....
A broad valley higher up than the main valley it leads into	....

[3]

(ii) Physical (natural) features provide opportunities for leisure.
     Explain how the area shown could be used for leisure activities.

[7]

(b) Study the map showing National Parks in England and Wales.

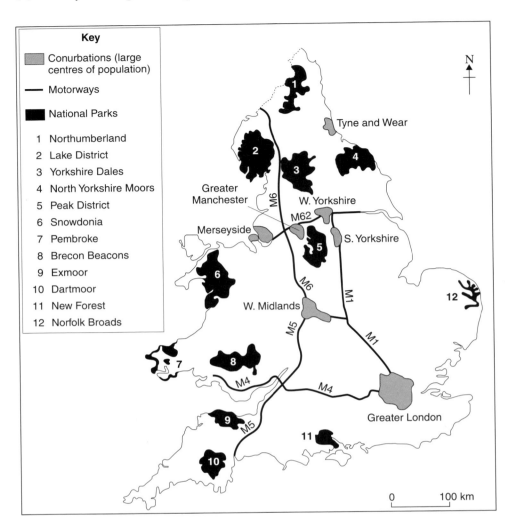

Key

Conurbations (large centres of population)

Motorways

National Parks

1 Northumberland
2 Lake District
3 Yorkshire Dales
4 North Yorkshire Moors
5 Peak District
6 Snowdonia
7 Pembroke
8 Brecon Beacons
9 Exmoor
10 Dartmoor
11 New Forest
12 Norfolk Broads

(i) State which National Park is surrounded by motorways and conurbations. [1]

(ii) National Parks attract many tourists. This may lead to land use conflicts with others such as farmers and landowners.

Using examples from your own studies, describe conflicts that may occur. [7]

(c) (i) Explain the meaning of 'tourist honeypot'. [3]

(ii) Name an example of a tourist honeypot which you have studied. Explain why it has become a tourist honeypot. [9]

SEG Specimen exam paper issued in 1996 for the 1998 examination

(any hints on answers on pages 155–156 are the sole responsibility of the authors and have not been provided or approved by the Group.)

Glossary

Accessibility   A measure of how easy – how fast and how cheap – it is to get to a place.

Added value   When goods are processed for sale, or simply packaged in a certain way, their value increases. Industry and trade depend on value-adding processes.

Agriculture   The basic primary industry and the source of food for the world's population.

Air mass   In north-west Europe, the weather is caused by air 'invading' from north, south, east or west. Invading masses of air come from particular source regions where the high-pressure air gathers particular characteristics. As air masses move from high-pressure to low-pressure areas we can predict the weather they will bring.

Amenities/facilities   Services provided for people in their homes or locality.

Atmosphere   The layers of air surrounding the Earth.

Biodiversity   The variety of species within an ecosystem.

Biomass   The weight of organic matter produced by the ecosystem. Ecosystems can be compared in terms of the increase in biomass per year.

Biome   The name for ecosystems on a global scale, such as deserts, rainforests and tundra.

Biosphere   The zone where life is found on the Earth.

Birth rate   A measure of the number of births in a year, usually expressed as a proportion per thousand of the total population.

Carnivore   Meat eater.

Carrying capacity   The maximum potential number of inhabitants that can be supported in an area.

CBD (central business district)   The space at or near the centre of a city which is occupied by shops, offices and other commercial functions.

City   Cities are urban places. They are usually large (more than 20,000 people) and are economically self-sufficient (unlike a large 'dormitory' or suburban town, for example).

Condensation   When water changes from a gas to a liquid as it cools.

Conservationist   Someone who has a concern for future developments and their impact on the physical environment. Conservationists are not against development; they are for development that is environmentally sustainable.

Consumer   Consumers are people. As trade in goods and services increases, the power of the consumer increases. Industries must create what people want (or think they need).

Costs   Expenses incurred in setting up or running an industrial activity.

Cycle   A series of events occurring in the same order each time.

Death rate   A measure of the number of deaths in a year, usually expressed as a proportion per thousand of the total population.

Deforestation   The clearance of forests.

Demographic Transition Model (DTM)   A model which tries to explain how populations change as they move through various stages of economic development.

Density   The number of people, houses or other items found within a given area.

Deposition   The dropping of material which has been picked up and transported by water, wind or ice.

Desertification   Dry ecosystems, particularly those on the edge of deserts, are fragile and can be turned into 'deserts' by the combined effect of natural and human impacts.

Discharge   The quantity of water flowing through a river or stream at a given time.

Drainage basin   The area drained by a river.

Drought   A long continuous period of dry weather.

Economic activity   Any human activity which involves the creation of wealth, e.g. farming, mining, factory production.

Economic development   The growth of an area's economy such as agriculture, industry or services.

Economy of scale   In the 20th century, one trend all over the world has been for industries to amalgamate (join, or grow bigger) so that they can buy and sell in bulk. Bulk operations are usually cheaper and therefore more profitable.

Ecosystem   The ecosystem is the most important idea in ecology. *Ecology* is the study of living things in their natural surroundings, or environment; it is about seeing and studying the whole picture as well as the pieces. An *ecosystem* is a certain area which contains living things that occupy habitats. It includes the rock, the soil and the air. It can be small (for example a duckpond) or very large (for example a desert).

Employment   The work people do to earn money and to sustain life:
- *Primary:* employment in industries that extract raw materials.
- *Secondary:* employment in industries that manufacture products.
- *Tertiary:* employment in service industries.
- *Quaternary:* employment in the new 'knowledge industries'.

Environmental determinism   The theory that people's behaviour is determined by the physical environment. Not many scientists now believe this theory to be true.

Erosion   This occurs when a moving agent (usually water) wears away and removes material. Breaking waves and running water cause much erosion.

EU (the European Union)   The group of fifteen European countries which try to promote common trading, economic and social policies.

Evaporation   When a liquid changes to a gas or vapour.

Evapotranspiration   Combined water loss from evaporation and transpiration.

Exports   Goods sent out of one country for sale in another country.

Flood   When a river overflows because it does not have sufficient space to hold all its discharge.

Flows   The links or transfers between parts of a system.

Fluvial processes   Processes associated with rivers.

Fold mountains   Perhaps the most dramatic evidence of action taking place at plate margins. The highest mountains are formed of crumpled sedimentary rocks, squeezed and folded by colliding plates.

Food web   All ecosystems include plants and animals that have feeding relationships. Such links can be displayed as a web or network or chain. The food web shows energy flows through the ecosystem.

Function   The function of something (for example a city) is what it does and how it works.

Global warming   Most scientists and politicians now agree that climates around the world are changing, probably because the Earth's 'greenhouse effect' is more efficient, preventing heat loss to outer space. Some meteorologists think that another result of global warming is more extreme weather events around the world, including in Britain: more droughts, more floods, stronger winds.

Gross domestic product (GDP)   A measure of national wealth, calculated by the value of goods and services produced by a country.

Gross national product (GNP)   The GDP of a nation together with any money earned from investment abroad. Usually divided by the country's population and expressed as 'per capita'.

Groundwater   The water found below the surface of the ground, beneath the water table.

Groundwater flow   The flow of water below the surface.

Growth rate   A measure of the increase in population, expressed as a percentage of the previous total population.

Habitat   The place where a plant, animal or organism normally lives.

Herbivore   Animals that eat plants.

Housing types   Classifying houses according to whether they are terraced, detached, semi-detached, etc.

Hydrograph   The graph which plots the discharge of a river.

Hydrological cycle   The continuous transfer and storage of water in the environment.

Hydrosphere   The water on the Earth.

Imports   Goods brought into a country from another country.

Indicators   Indicators are used to measure something indirectly.

Infiltration   The gradual seeping of water into the land.

Infrastructure   Roads, railways, airports, banks, energy and water supplies, law courts, schools and universities – it is the infrastructure of a country that can determine whether or not its economy will grow.

Inputs/outputs   Energy entering and leaving a system.

Interception   The holding of raindrops by plants as water falls on their leaves and stems.

Labour   The workers involved in production of goods and services.

Lag time   The length of time between peak rainfall and the peak discharge of a river.

Land use   The way space is used – the function of that space. Geographers draw maps of land use. The maps often show patterns of different land use. The patterns can sometimes reveal the economic, social and political processes that caused them.

Landform   A particular feature or shape of the land, for example a cliff, slope, or meander (bend of a river).

Landscape   A whole collection of features and shapes that make a complete pattern. When looking at landscapes we normally include human features as well as physical ones. Landscapes can be *managed* – in other words, people attempt to control physical processes to some extent. The most common examples are coastal protection and river flood protection.

LEDC (less economically developed country) Countries with a low GNP that are usually trying to boost their living standards by developing their resources.

Linkages   Connections between the different components in an economic system.

Lithosphere   The rocks of the Earth's crust.

Market economy   The 'market' is where goods and services are sold to consumers at competitive prices. Some countries are new to the market economy, such as Russia and China.

Mass movement   This takes place on slopes. All weathered material (rock broken up by the weather) moves downslope – sometimes by gravity, sometimes transported by agents of erosion (usually water). Mass movements can be sudden, as in a landslide.

MEDC (more economically developed country) Countries with a high GNP that have become wealthy by developing their industrial structure.

Migration   The movement of people, either within a country, or between countries.

Model   A simplified representation of the real world made in order to understand its workings.

Nutrients   Minerals that plants need for food.

Owner-occupied   Owner-occupied houses are occupied by the people who own them – usually with the help of a bank loan or mortgage.

Percolation   Gradual seepage of water down through the soil.

Permeable/impermeable   Allows/does not allow water to pass through.

Photosynthesis   The process by which green plants take in sunlight, carbon dioxide and water to produce oxygen, tissue and energy.

Physical processes   Processes at work in the atmosphere (air), hydrosphere (water) and lithosphere (rocks).

Plate   Vast, solid part of the Earth's crust, separated from other plates by fractures or plate boundaries.

Plate margin   The same as a plate boundary – this is where all the activity is.

Population density   The number of people in a certain area, usually expressed as the number of people per square kilometre.

Population structure   The proportions of a population in various age groups. The structure of population determines its needs. For example, as a young population grows older, it needs lots of schools.

Porous   Rocks able to hold water in pore spaces like a sponge.

Precipitation   The deposition of moisture from the atmosphere such as rain, hail, snow.

Primate city   Some countries have one city – the primate city – which, in terms of its population size and functions, dominates all other urban places.

Private rented   Private rented houses are occupied by people who pay a weekly or monthly rent to the owner.

Producers   Green plants that can turn the Sun's energy into plant food.

Quality of life   People have different levels of access to the 'good life' (a lifestyle that has a good quality).

Range of goods and services   Services with a high *threshold* usually have a large range – that is, the distance people are willing to travel to obtain that service.

Redevelopment   The demolition of old buildings and the replacement of them with new ones on the same site.

Relief   The shape of the Earth's surface.

Resources   These can be dead or alive, organic or inorganic – any part of the environment. Things become resources when people find a use for them (or when they realise how useful they are).

River   A permanent flow of water bordered by river banks.

Run-off   Movement of water over the surface of the land.

Rural   Rural lifestyles are found in the countryside: farms, villages and even small market towns have a rural setting rather than an urban one.

Scale   All maps have a scale. Geographers use maps to analyse issues and questions. Usually the scale of analysis determines what we can analyse. For example, how we describe a city depends on whether we examine it as a whole (small-scale map showing a large area), borough by borough (medium-scale map showing a smaller area), or by census ward (large-scale map showing a small area).

Sediment   Small particles worn away from the Earth's surface.

Services   The main function of cities is to provide services to people, such as places to work, shops, parks, etc.

Settlement hierarchy   In any region, settlements are arranged in different-sized groups, e.g. city, town, village, hamlet. One reason for this is that services also have a hierarchy. For example, there is need for only one regional shopping centre, but hundreds of 'corner shops'.

Socio-economic groups   Classification of people according to their occupation, for example professional, skilled, manual.

Soil erosion   Soil is a crucial part of ecosystems. It can be easily damaged, usually by running water or wind.

Special Economic Zones (SEZs)   These are found in countries all over the world, including China: special areas where taxes are low, planning controls and 'red tape' non-existent, and where industry can grow fast.

Spontaneous settlements   These develop in spaces without previous planning or preparations being made; individuals or groups settle here, sometimes illegally, because they need somewhere to live.

Stewardship   The idea that people are entrusted to look after the world for future generations.

Subsidy   Key industries, such as agriculture, sometimes receive money from the government to make sure they go on producing. Such industries are *subsidised*.

Suburbs   The outer rim of urban places.

System   A set of interrelated parts.

Tectonic processes   Earth-building processes of enormous power.

Tenure   How people occupy their homes such as owner-occupied or rented.

Threshold population   The minimum population required to provide enough customers to keep a shop (or service) in business.

Throughflow   Movement of water through the soil.

Tourism   The world's largest industry which itself supports a long list of other industries – travel, banking, restaurants, hotels, etc.

Transnational company (TNC)   A company which has factories and offices in several different countries. Such companies can move their workers and money around the world with ease.

Transpiration   Loss of water by plants to the atmosphere.

Tributary   A small river or stream that flows into a larger one.

Unemployment   Lack of paid work.

Urban area   A town or a city.

Urban structure   The way space is used in a city usually gives rise to an urban land use pattern, or structure.

Urbanisation   The growth of towns and cities and the movement of people away from rural living.

Water table   The level under ground, beneath which the rock is saturated.

Watershed   The boundary of a drainage basin.

Weather and climate   Data are collected daily on the results of atmospheric processes: temperature, humidity, precipitation, etc. These data can be averaged over a month to give a monthly summary for a place. The monthly averages for a place can be averaged for 30 years to give the average monthly conditions. The daily measurements are the *weather*. The 30-year averages show the *climate*.

Weathering   The breakdown of rocks by various forces.

Work   Any occupation, paid or unpaid.

Zone of transition   An area in which there is change.

Index

Acknowledgements

We are grateful to the following for permission to reproduce photographs:
AKG London, Figure 5.15; Ardea London, 4.1a (photo Lindau) and 5.27c (Steyn); Art Directors, 2.47 above and 2.53; John Birdsall Photography, page 4 below, 2.16 (semi-detached) and page 126(5); British Trust for Conservation Volunteers, page 4 above (Alexander); Britstock IFA, page 126(3) (Bach); J. Allan Cash Photolibrary, 2.31, 2.32 and 2.47 below left; Chilworth Media Associates, 3.14C and D (W.J.Allen); John Cleare Mountain Camera, 4.53, 5.29a and 5.31; Greg Evans International, 1.3 (Cullen); Ford Motor Company, page 126(1); Geoscience Features, page 66 above and 4.1b; Robert Harding Picture Library, 1.2, 1.15 (Atchison-Jones), 2.16 (detached and flats), 2.37a and b, 2.52 (Hawkins), 2.54, 5.29b (Rainford) and 5.29c (Francis); Grant Heilman Photography, 3.19 (Grant Heilman); Jane Herrington and Andy Beaumont, 2.13 (Grove), 2.14, 2.22, 3.12, 3.14a and b, 4.22, 4.23, 4.29, 4.30, 4.31 and 4.32; ICCE Photolibrary, 4.39 (Jacolyn Wakeford); Icelandic Photo Library, 4.3 (Palsson); Image Bank, page 60 above (Schon); Images of Africa, 2.50 and 5.27d (Jones); Ionica Cambridge, page 126(4); Link Picture Library, 5.27b (Eliason); Magnum Photos, 3.23 (Franklin); Peter Newark's American Pictures, 3.18; Oxford Scientific Films, 3.15 above (Dermid), 3.15 below (Cayless), 3.17 (Benvie) and 3.20 (Bannister); Panos Pictures, 3.28 (Sprague) and page 86 below right (Jones); Ross Parry Picture Agency, 4.16; Photo Researchers Inc, 1.16 (Warren), 2.35 (Corwin) and 3.24 (Fletcher and Baylis); Rapho Paris, 2.41 (Halary), 2.43a (Tostelin), 2.43b (Francy), 2.43c (Charles) and 2.43d (Poulsen); Rex Features, 4.15 (Sipa); Science Photo Library 1.10 (National Snow and Ice Data Center), 1.14 (Mead), 2.1 (W.T. Sullivan and Hansen Planetarium), 2.39 (CNES, 1993 Distribution Space Image), page 61 (Geospace), page 86a (US Department of Interior), page 86b (Bartel), page 86 centre right (Wood), 4.43 (Parker) and 4.48 (NRSC); Skyscan Balloon Photography, 2.13 (Spitalfields); Snowdonia National Park Authority, 5.32; Frank Spooner Pictures, page 126(2) (Gamma/Turpin), 5.16a and b (Gamma/Piel); Still Pictures, page 60 below (Pern), page 66 below (Murray), 3.7 (Parker), 3.27b (Edwards), 3.27c (Maier), 3.27d (Edwards), 3.27e (Harrison), page 86c (Schytte), page 86 above right (Ruoso) and 4.42 (Schytte); Travel Ink Photo Library, 2.5 (Seine/Lewis, Thames and Trafalgar Square/Cargill, Paris, Metro/Badkin, Louvre/Marks, London Underground/Jones) and 2.19 (Badkin); Trip Photographic Library, 4.52 (Jacobs) and 5.27a (Jacobs); Tropix Photographic Library, page 66 centre (Schmid) and 3.27a (Charlwood); Viewfinder Colour Photo Library, 2.16 (terraced/Murland) and 2.47 below right; David Williams Picture Library, 4.1c.

We should like to acknowledge the following sources of other copyright material:
Evening Standard/Solo, 5.4; Facts on File Ltd, 3.7; Geographical Magazine, pages 57, 76, 80; Guardian, 2.25, 4.56 (Paul Brown); HMSO, 3.16 (Soil Survey and Land Research Centre), 4.48 (Meteorological Office); Independent, 4.11 (Raymond Whitaker); MEG, pages 47, 160–2; Observer, 4.54; SEG, pages 163–4; Yorkshire Evening Post, 2.33; Yorkshire Evening Press, 2.33.

The maps in Figures 2.21, 2.22, 2.28, 4.19, 4.29–4.32 and 5.30 are reproduced from the Ordnance Survey 1:50,000 and 1:25,000 scale mapping with the permission of the Controller of Her Majesty's Stationery Office © Crown copyright (399671).

Every effort has been made to reach copyright holders; the publishers would be glad to hear from anyone whose rights they have unwittingly infringed.